74 4

8 18

5

23

90 52 7

46

30

98 19 89

10 75 24

67 3

9

85

35

University of Nebraska Press: Lincoln and London

Nebraska Football

James E. Sherwood

the Coaches   the Players   the Experience

Copyright 1987 by the University of Nebraska Press
All rights reserved
Manufactured in the United States of America

The paper in this book meets the minimum require-
ments of American National Standard for Information
Sciences – Permanence of Paper for Printed Library
Materials, ANSI Z39.48-1984.

Library of Congress Cataloging in Publication Data
Sherwood, James E. ; 1946–
Nebraska football.
Bibliography: p.
Includes index.
1. University of Nebraska – Lincoln – Football –
History.   I. Title.
GV958.U53S53   1987
796.332'63'09782293   86-30737
ISBN 0-8032-4157-7 (alkaline paper)

For Diane who always encouraged me to try

Contents

Preface

How fortunate is the individual who can combine work and play. To be able to labor and enjoy at the same time is rare in this life and something to be treasured.

I am a football fan. I have been a football fan since childhood. Growing up in the East, in the days before the American Football League, I was a Giants fan through and through. One of my earliest football memories is that of watching the New York Giants and Baltimore Colts playing for the NFL Championship in the famous overtime game of 1958. Even then I was hooked.

When the University of Nebraska Press approached me about writing a book on Cornhusker football, I jumped at the chance. This would allow me, a historian by training, to leave the archives and arcane minutiae which so often occupy the historian's time and delve into a phenomenon that has galvanized a state and captured the imaginations of countless thousands over five generations.

Not being a native Nebraskan, I came late to the "Big Red" legend. I would like to think that this gives me a different and, perhaps, a fresher perspective on the topic. Like Coach Bob Devaney, I too lived in Nebraska a while before I realized the Cornhuskers lost the 1941 Rose Bowl. I had heard of Sam Francis and George Sauer and Johnny Rodgers. I had seen the trophies in the South Stadium foyer. But, I hadn't met too many of the former players; certainly few of the stars. I was anxious to meet them, to speak with them and find out what it had been like to play against Red Grange; to try and stop the "Four Horsemen" of Notre Dame; to play against the Bud Wilkinson-coached Sooners; to try and stop Steve Owens or Billy Sims.

As I began interviewing former players for the book, I came to realize that these legends were something more than football heroes; something more than numbers on a program. They were people just like me. They had fun. They were afraid. They were enthusiastic. They were bored. Now the project took a twist. I wanted to convey this discovery to the reader. I wanted to shout that "football players are people too."

Several books have been written about Nebraska football fortunes. Some, of course, are better than others. Sometimes the stories have become clouded with age. Often there is disagreement between authors over certain incidents. I wanted to find out what happened. I wanted to go back and talk with the players, to look them in the eye and see what they saw, and, if possible, feel the crash of helmets, the thump of shoulder pads.

I met some great people in the course of this project. I enjoyed every interview and, when playing back the tapes, could still see the enthusiasm and pride that these men exhibited. Sed Hartman, living in a residential hotel for senior citizens, apologized for wearing glasses. He explained that he recently had surgery on his eye and was unable to wear his contacts. He didn't like the glasses because he felt they made him look old. Considering the humor in his voice, the twinkle in his eye, and a jaunty bow tie in his collar, I didn't feel he had any apologies to make. Although I knew when Sed had played for Nebraska, it wasn't until he began reminiscing about seeing Teddy Roosevelt campaign in 1912 and about playing against the "Four Horsemen" that it dawned on me how old Sed was.

Bob Mehring spent hours in the room off his living room that he uses for Nebraska memorabilia going through his scrapbooks with me, explaining photographs and telling stories. If I closed my eyes, Bob had me in Memorial Stadium waiting for D. X. Bible to send in substitutes or watching Lloyd Cardwell make another tackle.

Al Zikmund, busy in his duties as athletic director at Kearney State College, apologized ahead of time that he could only spare about a half an hour for an interview. That half hour stretched to an hour and then two and then almost three. When we finally concluded, he thanked me for helping him remember so many of the good times. I assured him that I was the one to offer thanks. His enthusiasm was almost contagious. I felt I knew what it was like to stand on the field in front of ninety thousand fans at the Rose Bowl and hope that Biff Jones had devised the right strategy for defensing the T formation. When Al came around his desk and got into a three-point stance, I could see the blond sophomore from Ord who was the fastest member of Nebraska's Rose Bowl team.

Adrian Fiala sat behind a big desk befitting the successful lawyer that he has become. But, as he leaned back, twisting the Big 8 Championship ring around and around on his finger, he was a kid again. A kid who was waiting for Coach Devaney to send him into a game. A kid who was trying to make a choice between Notre Dame and Nebraska and realizing that it could influence his entire life. Listening to Adrian laugh and then grow serious about his experiences, I recognized how much Nebraska football meant to him and still means to him.

In this, Adrian Fiala is a composite of the former Cornhuskers with whom I spoke. Most recognize that life goes on. They will never be children again. They will never run out into Memorial Stadium to the cheers of tens of thousands. But give them a moment to close their eyes and they are there. It is an experience that has shaped their lives and one that no one will ever be able to take from them.

Dictionaries define a legend as "a notable person or the stories of his exploits." Nebraska has had many legends since 1890. What follows is their story. A story we can all share and one in which we can find much to admire.

Anyone who has written a book knows how much is owed to others. From personal experience, I can attest to the fact that what follows on the succeeding pages has been improved by the judicious comments and suggestions of many people.

My colleagues in the Department of History at the University of Nebraska–Lincoln took time to read the manuscript as it was taking shape. Pete Maslowski, while never the most gentle of commentators, proved to be sharp-eyed and quick-triggered with the red pencil. His suggestion of a word here or a deletion there smoothed out the rough edges and made for a better manuscript. Dane Kennedy, still a Californian at heart, asked the questions that helped clarify the thinking of an author shrouded in the Big Red Mist. Ed Homze puffed on his pipe and posed problems and questions and offered needed encouragement.

I can't thank enough Ben Rader, also of the UNL History Department, who was responsible for interesting me in this undertaking in the first place. John Carter and his staff at the Nebraska State Historical Society helped me search out many of the old photographs that accompany the text. Joe Svoboda of the University of Nebraska Archives provided similar assistance. Also valuable were the private collections to which I was granted access. Bob Mehring's memories and photos have added much to the success of the project.

Speaking of photographs, words alone are inadequate for expressing my thanks for the countless hours put in by Dan Dulaney. I can assure the readers that the photographs by Dan that grace the pages of this book mark only a small fraction of the frames shot looking for just the right picture. Dan believes that out of every hundred frames shot there is maybe one usable photograph. A man of conviction, Dan was never hesitant about shooting one more roll of film in hope of a better picture.

Larry Young also deserves special mention. Larry was always willing to take a break in his own work to listen to an idea or look at a photograph. Larry proved that a good listener is a valuable asset indeed.

Finally, I have to thank the players and coaches, both present and past, who took the time to respond to my questionnaire and submit to interviews. Without them, there would be no book. I regret that I was unable to interview all the former Cornhuskers because I am sure that each would have had something to add to this story. However, various reasons and circumstances limited those with whom I was able to speak. A list of the players whose comments increased my knowledge of and, in many cases, admiration for the Nebraska football experience follows. The enthusiasm and honesty with which they answered my questions gave further evidence of the truth of a comment made by Al Zikmund: "Once you're a Cornhusker, you're always a Cornhusker."

PLAYERS INTERVIEWED

Clifford Ashburn	Larry Jacobson
Jack Ashburn	Craig Johnson
Marvin Athey	George Knight
James Baffico	Bill Kosch
Ritch Bahe	Edward Lanphere
Forrest Behm	Chuck Malito
Robert Benson	Bernie McGinn
William Berquist	Kent McCloughan
Clair Bishop	Bob Mehring
Wayne Blue	Fred Meier
Charles Bryant	Richard Moore
David Butterfield	Glen Munn
Lloyd Cardwell	Jerry Murtaugh
Pat Clare	James Myers
Dennis Claridge	Tom Novak
Dick Davis	Jack Pesek
Herbert Dewitz	Roy Petsch
Willard Dover	Warren Powers
Ted Doyle	Glenn Presnell
Fred Duda	Clarence Raish
Adrian Fiala	Steve Runty
Ken Fischer	Kelly Saalfeld
Pat Fischer	Carl Samuelson
Rex Fischer	Sam Schwartzkopf
Sam Francis	David Shamblin
Don Fricke	Paul Shields
Donald Glantz	Red Thibault
Michael Green	Richard Thompson
Lloyd Grimm	Fred Thomsen
Sed Hartman	Robert Thorton
Fred Hawkins	Harry Tolly
Clarence Herndon	LaVerne Torczon
Donald James Hewitt	Ed Weir
Ladas Hubka	Harold Wilder
Harold Hutchison	Tim Wurth
Guy Ingles	Al Zikmund

NEBRASKA FOOTBALL THROUGH THE YEARS

1890 First Nebraska football team

1893 Frank Crawford becomes coach (1893–94)

1895 Charles Thomas becomes coach

1896 Edward N. Robinson becomes coach (1896–97)

1898 Fielding H. Yost becomes coach

1899 A. E. Branch becomes coach

1900 W. G. Booth becomes coach (1900–1905)
First Nebraska squad to use nickname Cornhuskers

1906 Amos Foster becomes coach
Nebraska records victory number 100: Nebraska 17–Creighton 0

1907 W. C. Cole becomes coach (1907–10)

1910 Nebraska's largest victory margin: Nebraska 119–Haskell 0.

1911 Jumbo Stiehm becomes coach (1911–15)

1914 Vic Halligan named All-American (Nebraska's first)

1916 E. J. Stewart becomes coach (1916–17)

1918 W. H. Kline becomes coach

1919 Henry F. Schulte becomes coach (1919–20)

1921 Fred Dawson becomes coach (1921–24)

1923 Memorial Stadium opens
Nebraska records victory number 200: Nebraska 34–Kansas State 12

1925 Elmer Bearg becomes coach (1925–28)

1929 Dana X. Bible becomes coach (1929–36)

1937 L. McC "Biff" Jones becomes coach (1937–41)

1940 Nebraska records victory number 300: Nebraska 9–Pittsburgh 7

1941 Rose Bowl, Jan. 1. First

Nebraska bowl appearance:
Stanford 21–Nebraska 13
Nebraska records loss number 100: Indiana 21–Nebraska 13

1942 Glenn Presnell becomes coach

1943 A. J. Lewandowski becomes coach (1943–44)

1945 George "Potsy" Clark becomes coach

1946 Bernie Masterson becomes coach (1946–47)

1948 George "Potsy" Clark becomes coach (only man to serve two nonconsecutive terms as Nebraska coach)

1949 Bill Glassford becomes coach (1949–55)

1953 Sept. 19. Nebraska's first television appearance (carried on NBC): Oregon 20–Nebraska 12

1955 Orange Bowl, Jan. 1.
Nebraska's first Orange Bowl appearance:
Duke 34–Nebraska 7

1956 Pete Elliot becomes coach

1957 Bill Jennings becomes coach (1957–61)

1958 Nebraska records loss number 200: Purdue 28–Nebraska 0

1962 Bob Devaney becomes coach (1962–72)
Gotham Bowl, December 15.
Bob Devaney's first bowl team: Nebraska 36–Miami (Fl.) 34

1964 Nebraska records victory number 400: Nebraska 9–Missouri 0

1965 Cotton Bowl, Jan. 1.
Nebraska's first Cotton Bowl appearance: Arkansas 10–Nebraska 7

1967 Sugar Bowl, Jan. 2. Nebraska's first Sugar Bowl appearance: Alabama 34–Nebraska 7

1969 Sun Bowl, Dec. 20. Nebraska's first Sun Bowl appearance: Nebraska 45–Georgia 6

1970   Astro-Turf installed in Memorial Stadium
Cornhuskers are national champions

1971   Larry Jacobson awarded Outland Trophy
Cornhuskers are national champions

1972   Johnny Rodgers awarded Heisman Trophy
Rich Glover awarded Outland Trophy and Lombardi Trophy

1973   Tom Osborne becomes coach (1973–present)

1974   Largest Memorial Stadium crowd. Oklahoma 26–Nebraska 14

1975   Nebraska records victory number 500: Nebraska 63–Colorado 21
Fiesta Bowl, Dec. 26. Nebraska's first Fiesta Bowl appearance: Arizona State 17–Nebraska 14

1976   Astro-Bluebonnet Bowl, Dec. 31. Nebraska's first Astro-Bluebonnet Bowl appearance: Nebraska 27–Texas Tech 24

1977   Liberty Bowl, Dec. 19. Nebraska's first Liberty Bowl appearance: Nebraska 21–North Carolina 17

1981   Dave Rimington awarded Outland Trophy

1982   Dave Rimington awarded Outland Trophy and Lombardi Trophy. (Only individual to be recipient of two Outland Trophies)

1983   Mike Rozier awarded Heisman Trophy
Dean Steinkuhler awarded Outland Trophy and Lombardi Trophy

1985   Nebraska records victory number 600: Nebraska 41–Kansas State 3

The preceding list of significant dates in Nebraska football history is not meant to be all-inclusive. For a complete breakdown of chronological and statistical information on the Nebraska football program, consult the current edition of the *Nebraska Football Press Guide*, published annually by the Sports Information Department of the University of Nebraska–Lincoln.

§1

The History of the Huskers

1. Nebraska's first squad—the 1890 team. Courtesy of the Nebraska State Historical Society

Chapter One

The Early Years

In 1890 the University of Nebraska played its first football game, and since then life has never been the same in Big Red country.

The fielding of NU's first team did not take place without some encouragement from the student body. As early as 1883 the student newspaper, the *Hesperian*, had launched the drive to start a football team, proclaiming: "If a football team could be formed we might in years to come have enough college enthusiasm to designate ours a real college and not a gathering place for those who do not know what a live college should be." The newspaper maintained the pressure on the student body and the administration to support a team. By the end of the decade the newspaper was exalting over the fact that the university had purchased a football. The considered opinion of the editors was that this student purchase was "ugly and a daisy."

By 1890 the university enrolled about five hundred students and was ready for some competition. In a Thanksgiving Day contest the men from the university defeated the Omaha YMCA by a score of 10–0. A second victory followed in February 1891 over Doane College, 18–0. Doane fell again to the boys from Lincoln, 28–14, in November 1891. The *Hesperian* now decided that if the game was to be played it should be played properly. The paper discovered that such a decision involved money. In December, 1891 it editorialized: "The university is going at football in earnest and it is now necessary to clothe the team. Canvas suits for the eleven would cost a little over $35. Members of the faculty should dig in their pockets for funds."

Nebraska was simply joining in what had become a national trend. Ben Rader, a member of the History Department at the University of Nebraska, in his book *American Sports: From the Age of Folk Games to the Age of Spectators* (1983) found that "in the last three decades of the nineteenth century, football evolved from a simple informal diversion of a few young "gentlemen" in northeastern academies and colleges into a serious enterprise involving the student bodies, college authorities, alumni, and thousands of spectators." The figures bear out this assertion. Harvard University had begun to play football in

1874. On May 14, Harvard played a kind of rugby football against a team from McGill University of Canada and even charged fifty cents for admission. The following year Harvard and Yale University played their first game. Two thousand people paid fifty cents each to view the contest. In the 1880s and 1890s, Harvard and Yale met at the Polo Grounds in New York City for their annual contest. The reason was simple. The Polo Grounds would hold more people than any site on either campus. The need for the increased capacity is indicated by the crowds that attended the contests. In 1883 the game drew 10,000 spectators; in 1887, 24,000; and in 1891, 40,000 people packed into the game. Nebraska had a long way to go before it could match these figures.

Although the numbers might not be comparable to those of its eastern counterparts, the enthusiasm of the club fielded by the students of Nebraska was no less keen. Even the local papers were covering the squad's performances. Of course, sports writing was not yet the refined art it would become. The following account of the Nebraska-Iowa game in 1891 is an example. In an article datelined Omaha, November 26, 1891, the *Nebraska State Journal* provided this coverage:

There was a vast assemblage at the ball park this afternoon to witness the foot ball [sic] game between the Iowa state university and the university of Nebraska. The Iowa boys came in yesterday and had practice on the grounds in the afternoon. The Lincoln boys came up this morning, having done all their practice work at home. The committee in charge of the game did all in its power to advertise the game, and the different clubs interested came out in special conveyances, with all parts covered with ribbons and other ornaments. The two teams engaged in some preliminary practice work, and it was soon evident that the Nebraska boys had not the benefits of as efficient practice as their opponents. The Iowa rush line was also the heavier, but not as much as would be judged by casual observation, as they were heavily padded, which protection their opponents had not taken advantage of. At different times the crowd pressed upon the grounds to such an extent that the game had to be stopped to push them back and especially was this true during the latter part.

Even though Nebraska lost the game 22–0, as with all local reporting throughout the years the reporter had to end his article with a positive comment about the home team: "The game was not so one-sided as the score would indicate. Iowa had to win her ground by slow degrees, and admitted that the Nebraska boys were worthy opponents."

Following a loss to Doane College in December 1891, the editor of the *Hesperian* felt compelled to counsel the student body with a philosophy that would appear out of place today: "Probably it's better not to win all the time." Had that editor known that Nebraska squads in succeeding decades would win over six hundred college games he might not have felt the need to be so philosophical.

More and more students became involved in the game. Roscoe Pound, who would later gain fame as dean of Harvard Law School and as a noted jurist, was an official at the NU-Illinois game of 1892. This was Nebraska's first win over a major state university (6–0) and Pound refereed the first half and then traded with a fellow from Illinois to be the umpire in the second half. By 1895, Willa Cather and Dorothy Canfield won the University Literary Club's first prize with a piece about football. In the same year, Pound authored a piece in Latin on the football team. One later commentator remarked that "the sport survived both literary efforts."

Fan involvement was also on the increase. Behavior that would be common at more recent Nebraska games was already present. In an article describing the 1892 Illinois game, the *Nebraska State Journal* noted, "Red neckties were common. One fellow wore a vest half red, half white." Its description of the Kansas game of the same year also took notice of fans' attire. "The university colors of scarlet and cream were displayed in all the usual and a few unusual ways. One of the unusual was the wearing of scarlet fezes with white tassels."

Reporters of the day were very much concerned with events surrounding the game, rather than concentrating solely on the game itself. In a report on Nebraska's loss the previous day to the Denver Athletic Club, the *Nebraska State Journal* for October 30, 1892, had a subheading that read "Beaten Badly, But Treated Nicely," and, in an article of two and a half paragraphs, found time to inform its readers that "members of the visiting eleven are well pleased with the treatment they have received at the hands of the Denver Athletic Club. They quartered the Nebraska team at the Brown Palace hotel and this evening both teams attended in a body the performance of the Lillian Russell Opera Company at the Tabor Grand."

The concern for accommodations and treatment extended to teams that visited Lincoln too. In its report on the Kansas game mentioned above, the same newspaper felt it important to note: "The Kansas team remained at the Lindell last night, and will leave for Lawrence at 7:45 this morning. They made many friends while here."

The first half of the 1890s produced many changes for Nebraska football and some for the game itself. On December 28, 1891, the Universities of Nebraska, Kansas, Iowa, and Missouri formed the Interstate League at a meeting in Kansas City. The intention of the founders was to facilitate scheduling and offer some stability and governance in a sport that was lacking in both. The Interstate League never lived up to these lofty expectations.

An incident that took place in 1892 provides evidence of the League's incapacity. In the final game of the 1891 season, George Flippin played left halfback for Nebraska. David Israel, in *The Cornhuskers: Nebraska Football,* pointed out what was so startling about this. "He [Flippin] was, as far as anyone can tell, the first black ever to play major college football." In 1892 Flippin was once again a member of the squad. The University of Missouri forfeited an Interstate League contest to Nebraska because Missouri would not play against a team fielding a black player.

Coaches at the University of Nebraska probably celebrate 1893 as a special year in the development of the NU program. In that year Nebraska had its first salaried head coach. Frank Crawford was paid the magnificent sum of $500 for directing the players' efforts. He was interested in a career in medicine and school officials encouraged him to take some of his salary in the form of free tuition. Even though Crawford substituted some of the tuition for cash and even though, for the first time, fans had to pay admission to Nebraska home games, the athletic association still wound up the season approximately $200 in debt.

To put the Nebraska financial effort in perspective, one need only consult some of the facts presented in Ben Rader's book. In 1892 the University of Chicago had awarded professorial rank to Amos Alonzo Stagg, the first coach in the United States to be so designated. By 1897 Yale was paying Walter Camp $1,750 to coach its football team. Perhaps even more telling is the note that in the early 1890s Yale paid $300 to purchase a mascot—an English bulldog. All this, taking place at a time when Nebraska couldn't meet the salary of its first paid coach, illustrates how the balance of football power has shifted in the twentieth century.

Along with a salaried coach, other changes were also in the works in Lincoln. In 1894 the football team accepted a challenge from the Butte Athletic Club to meet in a football contest. The Nebraska team readily accepted and traveled to Montana, where it lost 16–6. The defeat was saddening enough, but the reception the squad received upon its return to campus was even more shaking. Representatives of the faculty were outraged that students would miss five days of classes to travel to and from a "game" and demanded that the administration institute a policy to prevent such occurrences in the future. The administration found merit in the faculty's protest and established guidelines whereby faculty members would have to approve each year's football schedule. This was the beginning of the Faculty Athletic Committee at the university. According to David Israel, "And so it was that year that football became an integral part of university life."

The University of Nebraska has had its share of famous coaches over the years. In the 1890s two coaches who would earn niches in the National Football Hall of Fame spent time on the Lincoln campus. Edward North Robinson was head coach in 1896 and 1897 before heading east to Brown

University, and he was succeeded by an even more famous personage, Fielding "Hurry Up" Yost, who lasted only one season (1898) in Lincoln before moving on to rival Kansas University. It would be his exploits at the University of Michigan that would gain Yost his enshrinement.

The end of the century also marked the end of the Interstate Conference. In 1897 Iowa withdrew from the league, and in 1898 the conference played its last season. Nebraskans weren't too sorry to see the demise of the group. It had never provided the benefits that the original members had hoped and had pretty well existed as a league in name only.

The twentieth century began with the university attempting to improve its football organization. Three major steps were undertaken. Nebraska wanted a league affiliation and continued to search for the right partners. In 1901 the university applied for, and was denied, membership in the Big Nine, the predecessor of the Big Ten. A similar application was rejected in 1912. This search for partners was finally rewarded on January 12, 1907, when Nebraska became a charter member of the Missouri Valley Intercollegiate Athletic Conference. At a meeting in Kansas City, the Universities of Nebraska, Missouri, Iowa, and Kansas, as well as Washington University of St. Louis, formed the league, the principles of which were modeled on those of the Big Nine. A report in the *Nebraska State Journal* expressed hope that additional members might be found. Among the possible candidates were Iowa State

2. The 1894 team. George Flippin is in the second row, third player from the left. The team captain was George Henry Dern (second row, holding the ball). He would later serve as Secretary of War under President Franklin D. Roosevelt (1933–36). Courtesy of the University of Nebraska Archives

Agricultural College, Kansas State Agricultural College, Drake University, Washburn College, and the Universities of Oklahoma and Arkansas.

A major football program requires a suitable nickname. In 1900 the university officially adopted the nickname "Cornhuskers," agreeing with its originator, Cy Sherman, that it was a much better name than the previous one, the "Bugeaters." The third step of major significance was the hiring of Walter Cowles Booth as head coach. "Bummy" Booth had played his collegiate football at Princeton and was expected to bring the sophistication of eastern college football to the Great Plains. In return for meeting these expectations, Booth was offered a salary of $600 a year.

In the six years he was at Nebraska, Booth far exceeded the hopes of those who had hired him. He established the second highest winning percentage of any Nebraska coach (.861) as he won 52 games, lost 8, and tied 1. His 1902 team was not only undefeated but also unscored upon. By the 1904 season, his teams had put together a 27-game winning streak, the longest in Nebraska history. Although his 1905 team lost to both Michigan and Minnesota, it also set the still-standing record for highest combined score by NU and an opponent when it defeated in-state rival Creighton 102–31. Frederick Ware, the famed sports columnist of the *Omaha World Herald*, noted the impact Booth's teams had on the state. "First Nebraska the state stirred. Then Nebraska, bedazzled, blinked. And then Nebraska uttered a mighty cry of loyalty and pride, and demanded The Team for its own."

As so often happens in big-time sports, finances reared their ugly heads. "Bummy" Booth felt that he should be rewarded for his accomplishments and the administration agreed. The problem was that Booth and the administration couldn't agree on what constituted a suitable reward. Booth almost left after the 1904 season but when informed that his replacement would be someone who had played at Yale he elected to stay. Supposedly, Booth could not stand the thought of a Yalie replacing him at the helm. Not even the Princeton-Yale rivalry could keep Booth on campus after the 1905 season. When he departed for more opportune surroundings, Booth was making a little over $2,000 a year.

After a one-year stint as head coach by Amos Foster, who engineered Nebraska's 100th victory in the 17–0 defeat of Creighton University, Nebraska found an individual with a nickname almost as colorful as that of "Bummy" Booth and a coaching record nearly as enviable. W. C. "King" Cole took over the program in the 1907 season and spent the next four years leading the Scarlet and Cream to a combined record of 25–8–3. His winning percentage of .736 would be impressive in any circle and appears less so at Nebraska in this period only because of comparisons with Booth's. He would even surpass Booth's offensive accomplishments. Cole's 1910 squad managed to set the record for the most points ever scored by Nebraska against an opponent.

Haskell fell to the Cornhuskers 119–0. By the time Cole left the university, his salary was $3,000 a year.

Following Cole's departure, one of the most memorable periods in Nebraska football history began as Ewald O. Stiehm came to town. When a coach has a last name that is pronounced "Steam" and his team racks up victory after victory, what else could that team be called but the "Stiehm Rollers"? As a coach, "Jumbo" Stiehm brought glory and recognition to the Nebraska program in the form of five conference titles in five years and victories over nationally acclaimed teams. To some, the most impressive factor in these victories is that no Stiehm-coached team averaged even 160 pounds a man, which is far from the modern conception of a steamroller.

During the Stiehm years, the accomplishments of the team become almost too numerous to mention. For instance, an undefeated string began that wouldn't be halted until E. J. Stewart had replaced Stiehm in 1916. When the University of Kansas finally halted the streak, Nebraska had won 34 straight games dating back to 1912. Under Stiehm, Nebraska recorded one of its more notable victories. In 1915 Nebraska defeated Notre Dame, already the epitome of college football, by a score of 20–19. The next day, the *New York Times* declared: "With the win over Notre Dame, Nebraska definitely

3. A "charging machine"—1906, not the most sophisticated of equipment. Courtesy of the Nebraska State Historical Society

has come of age. It must be ranked with the major powers." Also under Stiehm's tutelage the University of Nebraska had its first All-American. Vic Halligan, a tackle, started what would be a long line of Nebraska players to be so honored.

Among the memories of the Stiehm years, one endures most vividly. Stiehm coached the athlete whom many, even today, consider the greatest ever to wear the Nebraska uniform: Guy Chamberlin. Chamberlin's accomplishments are legendary, but one writer has offered the most telling assessment. John McCallum, in his *Big Eight Football*, pointed out, "From prep school to the Cornhuskers and through his first five seasons as a professional, Chamberlain [sic] did not play in a losing game." Most athletes would tell you that they most value the respect of their teammates. Guy Chamberlin certainly had that. When asked in 1985 who he thought was the greatest player ever to wear a Nebraska uniform, Paul Shields, who played with Chamberlin for the Cornhuskers, responded: "Guy Chamberlin by a large margin. His running and carrying the ball was really something to behold, and as he also played end on defense, he likewise was a beautiful performer."

Chamberlin grew up in Blue Springs and Beatrice, Nebraska. "Grew up" is the proper phase too, because by the time he started playing college ball he stood 6′1″ and weighed a very solid 190 pounds. He spent his first two years of college at Nebraska Wesleyan University in Lincoln. Being the competitor he was, Chamberlin recognized after his sophomore year that there were no more worlds to conquer in small-college ball and transferred to the University of Nebraska. The NU coaching staff and players who had seen him in action for Nebraska Wesleyan aided and abetted this transfer. No National Collegiate Athletic Association existed in those days to monitor contacts with players and to regulate tampering. Players from Nebraska literally laid siege to the Chamberlin farm over the summer of 1913 to convince Guy to attend NU. Chamberlin would never regret the move.

The victory over Notre Dame in 1915 offered Chamberlin a showcase for his talents. An assistant coach from Notre Dame by the name of Knute Rockne had scouted the Cornhuskers and had witnessed some of Chamberlin's feats. However, his report assured the Notre Dame squad that he, Rockne, had discovered Chamberlin's weakness. According to Rockne, Chamberlin would never cut back against the grain of the pursuit. The key then was for Notre Dame's defense to chase after Guy with abandon, preventing him from breaking off any long runs. It didn't take Chamberlin long to recognize Notre Dame's strategy and begin cutting back against the grain. It's too bad there aren't any pictures of Rockne as he watched Chamberlin take off on long run after long run against the Irish defense. An appreciative audience looked on as Chamberlin performed his magic. On that October afternoon eight thousand spectators, the largest crowd in Nebraska football history to

4. Vic Halligan,
Nebraska's first All-
American. Courtesy of
the Nebraska State
Historical Society

that time, paid a then-record $11,768 to cheer their Scarlet and Cream on to victory.

Had Rockne read Stiehm's comments on his star player, he would not have been so quick to instruct the Irish defense. James Denney, in *Go Big Red*, quotes "Jumbo" as evaluating Chamberlin this way: "He is a wonderful player, with a combination of speed, weight and aggressiveness. He can plunge through the almost unmovable line, skirt the best of ends, or stop the most terrific runners while on defense. He has a quick head and is shifty enough to take advantage of every opportunity." Could a coach ask anything more of a player?

Newspaper reports of the contest document the importance of Chamberlin to the Cornhusker cause. The accounts in the *Omaha World-Herald* are particularly interesting because the author of the article, Miles Greenleaf, didn't have too much else good to say about the boys from Lincoln. Greenleaf noted, "That the score was not much larger for the Cornhuskers and much smaller for the South Benders, is altogether the fault of quarterback Caley [J. L., the NU quarterback], or whoever instructed him in not calling for more open plays and forward passes." At another point the reporter commented,

From the moment of the kickoff it seemed that Notre Dame would likely humble the Nebraska colors, for their line looked like a row of freight cars and their secondary defense was as fast as the United States mail. When upon the offensive play they had the most perfect interference ever seen on Nebraska Field and when defending their own colors they broke up play after play for Quarterback Caley, who could not seem to gather the thought into his bosom that the South Bend line was a thing of bulk and brawn and not to be tampered with."

Miles Greenleaf was a stern critic of all except Chamberlin. When it came to the play of the Nebraska left end, the reporter couldn't find enough words of praise for his actions. "Chamberlin was the whole show for the Lincolnites scoring two of their touchdowns against open fields that seemed impossible of penetration. His defensive stunts bordered on the miraculous while his open field running brought victory to the colors of the Cornhuskers." Later in the article, Greenleaf had to resort to a literary allusion to make his point, but still couldn't resist a dig at the Cornhusker game plan:

Chamberlain, like the warriors in the 'Charge of the Light Brigade' vainly hurled himself time after time against the human ice wagons of the foe. When it came to straight football the Notre Dame boys, sportsmen and heavyweights through and through, played like demons in both departments of the game, but when Nebraska opened up they were bewildered and this bewilderment took a long time in sinking into the minds of the men who bossed the Cornhuskers.

Following his All-America days at Nebraska, Guy went on to a successful professional career with the Canton Bulldogs, Chicago Staleys, and Frankfort Yellowjackets.

As had been the case with some of his predecessors, the issue that ended Stiehm's relationship with the University of Nebraska was money. After his success of 1915, the University of Indiana approached Stiehm. The "Hoosiers" offered "Jumbo" an annual salary of $4,500, approximately $1,000 more than he had been making at Nebraska. Being an honorable man, and enjoying his stay at the university, Stiehm gave the Athletic Association the opportunity to match the offer. Although it couldn't raise that much, the Association could come close. It offered Stiehm a new contract calling for an annual salary of $4,250. This was enough for the coach and he decided to stay. Feelings of relief spread across Nebraska until the university faculty intervened. Faculty members approached the administration, protesting the coach's new contract. They presented the argument that no football coach's salary should exceed that of a university professor. After a protracted argument, the faculty won out and the Athletic Association rescinded the offer to Stiehm. Faced with this reality, "Jumbo" went off to Indiana.

For the next two years, Nebraska maintained a successful program, winning the Missouri Valley Conference crown in 1916 and 1917, under Coach E. J. "Doc" Stewart. The 1917 squad was so good that it broke the century mark in a game against Nebraska Wesleyan, winning 100–0. Following Stewart, the seasons were not what Nebraska fans had come to expect. W. G. Kline's team posted a losing record, falling to such opponents as Iowa, Camp Dodge, and Washington University while salvaging a tie with Notre Dame and scoring wins over Kansas and the always tough Omaha Balloon School.

Henry F. "Pa" Schulte came along the next year and could manage only a 3–3–2 record. His 1920 squad did get the twentieth century's third decade off on the right foot by turning in a winning season (5–3–1) and setting the stage for what was to come. Over the next four seasons, Schulte's successor, Fred T. Dawson, would produce three Missouri Valley championships, memorable victories over nationally ranked opponents, and one of NU's most beloved All-Americans. It was during Dawson's tenure at Nebraska, in the 1924 season, that the football crowd surpassed 100,000 in attendance for the first time.

Dawson's first two teams each went 7–1. Each team's loss came on the road. In 1921 Notre Dame pulled out a 7–0 victory and in 1922 Syracuse overcame the Cornhuskers 9–6. Both the 1921 and the 1922 teams were conference champions, as was the 1923 squad. The 1923 team was the one that christened the new Memorial Stadium with the less than resounding 0–0 tie with the University of Kansas. If the fates weren't on the Cornhuskers' side in that contest, the other 1923 game against a Kansas rival showed that the Huskers hadn't been completely abandoned. The 34–12 victory over Kansas State University was the 200th win in Nebraska's history.

The 1923 season was an interesting one for Nebraska football fans. Anticipation created by the new stadium plus the enthusiasm for a topnotch schedule that included not only the traditional league opponents but such nonconference foes as Notre Dame, Illinois, and Syracuse had the faithful anxious for the fall. Before even the first practice, the *Lincoln Star* had articles reporting on the upcoming season. Cy Sherman, the paper's sports editor, on September 2 informed his readers that Nebraska and Illinois had come to an understanding to help prepare for the season's opening game between the schools. "The

5. The final home game
in the old stadium,
Thanksgiving Day, 1922.
Courtesy of the Nebraska
State Historical Society

6. The oratory was
stirring at the ground-
breaking ceremonies for
Memorial Stadium.
Courtesy of the Nebraska
State Historical Society

agreement of Dawson and Zuppke [the Illinois coach] to exchange formations in advance of the game has excited both wonderment and criticism, but both coaches probably had their hats on straight when they framed their pact. Each, for instance, is anxious that his protégés may have the benefits of stiff competition early in the season by way of preparing for future conference foes." Imagine Tom Osborne and Joe Paterno exchanging diagrams of their offensive and defensive formations prior to a Nebraska–Penn State game.

On September 30, Sherman reported that the plan to exchange formations had fallen through:

Announcement was made a few days ago that Coach Fred Dawson of Nebraska and Coach Bob Zuppke of Illinois had abandoned their plans to exchange charts of formations in advance of the fray at Urbana. Instead, it was explained, the two mentors had mutually entered into a new agreement, the exact nature of which could not be divulged. The secret popped loose, however, when Bert Ingwerson, former Illinois captain and present freshman coach at the Urbana institution, showed up in a seat in the west stand and busily made notes of every Cornhusker move. Simultaneously, Owen Frank, backfield coach at Nebraska, was at Urbana yesterday witnessing the clash of Zuppke's varsity aggregation and Ingwerson's yearlings, taking notes quite as industriously as the Illinois scout was doing here in Lincoln.

Unfortunately, all the preparations went for naught for the Cornhuskers. When the two teams finally met in Urbana on October 6, the Illini walked away with a 24–7 win.

In initiating plans to construct a new stadium, Nebraska was once again part of a national trend. Colleges all across the country were in a race to build stadiums to house their football teams. Much of this construction was undertaken in the name of praising American boys who had given their lives in World War I, hence the common name "Memorial Stadium," but it also provided an opportunity to showcase the increasingly popular football teams.

In Lincoln, groundbreaking for the new structure took place on April 26, 1923. At the ceremony, restraint was not the key word. One speaker waxed eloquent:

And is it not worth while to put Nebraska on the athletic map? This stadium will be notice to all the world that we are here prepared to receive all calls of friendship and of contest on a field the equal of any in the land. A record broken here will flash the champion's name to the utmost corners of the earth.

Then blow ye the trumpets! Send forth a challenge to the world! Come East! Come West! Come North! Come South! Come any part of the great round the globe, and Nebraska will give you welcome. Come giants of brawn! Come sprinters of speed! Come champions crowned with your unbroken record of victory on every field of honor, and Nebraska will meet you on equal terms in this arena.

Contributions from friends of the university, alumni, corporate sponsors, and anyone else willing to give provided the financing for this magnificent stadium. The Alumni Association organized a massive campaign designed to reach every possible donor. All sorts of exhortations went out by mail to keep the drive alive. For instance, right after the groundbreaking, an appeal was made that began: "Work on the Stadium has started—you can see the results of your pledge. Your investment is beginning to materialize. 70,000 yards of dirt are to be moved, more than four square blocks have been cleared, a railroad spur four blocks long is being laid, the contractors will soon be pouring concrete. All of this takes money."

The appeals were quite successful. Contributions rolled in, some small and some large, but the totals met the need. In the end, faculty contributed $25,000, students $122,000, fans from Lincoln $176,000, fans from Omaha $40,000, fans from the rest of Nebraska $60,000, and out-of-state fans $25,000. Since support from the state legislature was small, these private contributions were a necessity.

By fall the local newspapers were full of stories about the new stadium and speculation was rife about whether it would be ready for the scheduled opening. The squad assembled for practice on September 15 and amid all the preparations, with carpenters and workmen running about, forty men held the first workout in the new stadium. On September 24, Cy Sherman attended a scrimmage. In his article on the practice, Sherman noted, "The new field is far from being in shape for the pigskin pastime, as the soft footing slowed down the offensive efforts of both varsity and 'Frosh'."

Meanwhile, on September 16 the *Nebraska State Journal* printed a schematic of the stadium and included some interesting statistics for the edification of its readers. "If the seats in the stadium were placed end to end they would reach 8.52 miles. The height is 72 feet or as high as the average six story building. The seating capacity is 30,000 with arrangements whereby this can be increased to 47,000. It is one and one half city blocks long (476 feet) and half a block wide (136 feet)."

Following the season's opening loss to the University of Illinois, the Cornhuskers had a home game scheduled against the University of Oklahoma. The official dedication was not for another two weeks, preceding the Kansas game, but would the stadium be ready? Cy Sherman, in a Wednesday column, pointed out that it really didn't matter. "Although the stadium gridiron is soft and not in condition for fast football, the Huskers will use the field next Saturday for the obvious reason that they have no other."

After having been somewhat pessimistic about the stadium's readiness to

host a football game, Sherman's column on the Saturday contest, won by
Nebraska 24 to 0, had nothing but praise for the facility. Looking back, it also
demonstrated a real insight into the future of football at the university. Sherman wrote:

*Fifteen thousand spectators, the greatest gathering at an opening game in
Cornhusker history, witnessed the Sooner defeat. The verdict was general that
when the upper balconies and stadium walls are completed and a grass gridiron provides the proper setting in the middle of the bowl, football at Nebraska
will become a spectacle, rather than a game—a spectacle which will so appeal
to the followers of the pigskin sport as to regularly pack the stadium at all
important contests of the home schedule.*

Aside from the festivities celebrating the opening of the stadium, the
biggest home game of the year was Notre Dame's appearance in Lincoln.
Knute Rockne had his troops fresh and ready to put another mark in the W
column for the "Fighting Irish." The odds certainly looked stacked against the
Cornhuskers. The Irish were talented, experienced and deep. When Nebraska
had reported for its first practice of the season on September 15, Coach
Dawson was happy to suit up 40 players. Notre Dame opened its fall practice
the same day and Rockne welcomed 101 candidates.

If the disparity in numbers wasn't enough to bring an element of doubt to
the minds of Nebraska fans, the Cornhuskers' record that season wouldn't
inspire a great deal of confidence. After the opening loss to Illinois, the victory
over Oklahoma, and ties with Kansas at home and Missouri on the road, the
team had a record of 1–1–2. Local sports writers noted an air of overconfidence as the Notre Dame team came to town. Writing in the *Omaha World-
Herald* on the day of the game, Greg McBride noted, "There is no doubt that
the Notre Dame squad is taking Nebraska with a more or less sort of indif-
ferent over-confidence. The news carried back by Notre Dame scouts that
Notre Dame 'was four touchdowns better than the Nebraskans' may have
done its work."

One of those tired clichés would seem appropriate here. Something like
"when these two teams meet, you can throw out the records." The Dewitz
brothers, Rufus and Herb, led the Huskers to a 14–7 victory. Rufus threw a
touchdown pass and Herb kicked both points. Herb Dewitz has many fond
memories of this game and the team. To this day, he, like many players
interviewed for this book, considers the victory over Notre Dame the greatest
in Nebraska history. This is not an opinion formed by the dimmed memories
of past events. The headline in the *Nebraska State Journal* for Sunday,
November 11, 1923, proclaimed: "Husker Win Upsets World of Football." In
the article that followed, John Bentley offered his evaluation. "Saturday's

game will be written into one of the most glorious pages of Cornhusker football history. Coming out of oblivion and striking down what has been conceded the greatest football team in America this season is an afternoon's work which should brighten the log of any institution."

Sed Hartman, who lettered for three seasons as a running back under Fred Dawson, has a theory about why the Huskers won that day. The key, for Hartman, was Dawson's oratorical skills. "He [Dawson] was a talker, a very good talker. The sort of man who could build up the game very well. Against Notre Dame, I thought he was going to go crazy the way he talked. He'd build up the thing so high that everyone was ready to do anything for him when they went out on the field."

With the benefit of hindsight, Nebraskans can be even more impressed with this win. The Notre Dame backfield was composed of four juniors by the names of Miller, Crowley, Layden, and Stuhldreher. The following year, Grantland Rice would immortalize these individuals with the famous article beginning, "Outlined against a blue-gray October sky, the Four Horsemen rode again." The Cornhuskers had managed to keep the legendary Four Horsemen of Notre Dame under tight rein.

The Notre Dame game of 1923 was also the first game against the Fighting Irish for a man who would become a colossal thorn in the side of Knute Rockne. Rockne shouldn't have felt bad about this because Ed Weir did not seem partial to Notre Dame. Every Nebraska opponent would be forced to try and defense this man and few would ever come to any workable solution. Weir was a year away from his first of two All-American seasons in this 1923 game but still managed to demonstrate the talent that would eventually get him selected as Nebraska's first representative on Walter Camp's All-America team.

Ed had some of his best games against the University of Illinois. As with all great athletes, it may have been the challenge of playing against the best that caused him to reach such heights. Red Grange would have been challenge enough for any defense. When people think of college football in the 1920s, the "Galloping Ghost" is usually the first name that comes to mind. Mention Red Grange to a true Nebraska fan and he will probably tell you that Nebraska held Grange to one of his worst days as a collegian. In 1925, Grange left the game at the beginning of the fourth quarter almost in a state of tears because of the frustrations caused by the Cornhusker defense. In a 1962 column for the *Lincoln Journal*, Dick Becker recounted a story about the contests between Weir and Grange. Becker was quoting C. C. Frazier of Lincoln as he told the tale: "Ed was on the train from Lincoln to Lafayette, Ind., and I was heading for Indianapolis. Ed and I fell into conversation and I said: 'Ed, how did you stop Red Grange?' His answer was, 'I waited to see which way he was going and then I took after him.' It was just that simple." Tells you something

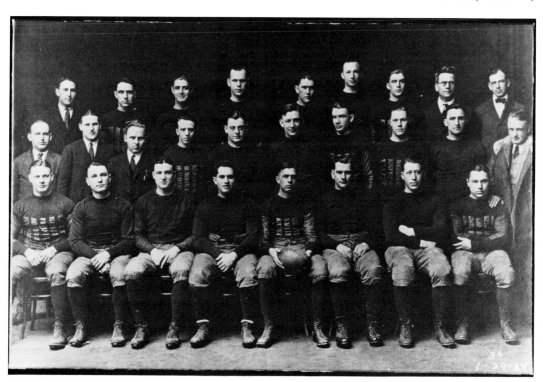

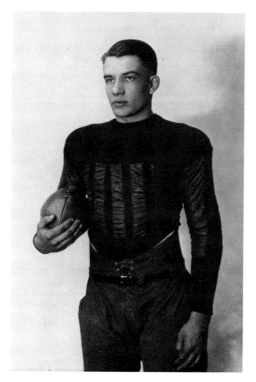

7. Fred Dawson's 1923 squad that scored the surprising victory over Notre Dame. Sed Hartman is the first player on the left in the first row. Courtesy of the Nebraska State Historical Society

8. Everyone's All-American, Ed Weir. Courtesy of the Nebraska State Historical Society

about Ed, doesn't it? What's that old cowboy expression—'No brag, just fact'. Ed proved that fact again and again for the Cornhuskers and then went on to a professional career with the Frankfort Yellowjackets.

Nebraska was becoming accustomed to winning, and winning in a big way. The 1924 season had ended with a 5–3 record for the Cornhuskers and the losses to Notre Dame, Illinois, and Oklahoma were enough to make the administration ask for Dawson's resignation. It wanted to replace him with a man with a national reputation, Bob Zuppke of Illinois. Zuppke wasn't interested, but did recommend the individual who would become Dawson's successor, Elmer E. Bearg.

Bearg was a serious sort of fellow who liked his football kept as simple as possible. You have bigger players than your opponent and you hit him harder than he hits you. Deception was a word not in Bearg's vocabulary. In four seasons at NU Bearg could do no better than match Dawson's record. Of course, when one considers that Dawson's record over four seasons was 23–7–2 for a winning percentage of .750 and Bearg's, for the same number of seasons, was 23–7–3 for a percentage of .736, one has to conclude that neither man had anything of which to be ashamed. To be picky, in one area Dawson was Bearg's superior. Dawson managed to bring three league championships to Lincoln while Bearg brought only one.

The one league championship secured by Bearg's team was a memorable one. The University of Nebraska had been searching for the perfect league. The Missouri Valley Conference was proving unsatisfactory for a number of reasons and so, on May 19, 1928, representatives from several colleges met in Lincoln. At this meeting, the Universities of Nebraska, Oklahoma, Missouri, and Kansas, along with Kansas State and Iowa State Universities, agreed on the formation of the Big Six Conference. Nebraska had finally found a home, one from which it would not stray over the next six decades. In looking back over the happy relationship NU has had with this league, it somehow seems fitting that the Cornhuskers captured the first league football championship.

Chapter Two

A Decade of Achievement

The thirties for many were one of the worst times in American history. Soup kitchens, bread lines, and unemployment were the norm throughout the country. In the Midwest, it was the time of the Dust Bowl, farm foreclosures, and broken dreams; the time of the Great Depression. One activity in the Midwest, however, was thriving, growing, prospering during this time. Bucking the trend, Nebraskans had found something of which to be proud; something to take their minds off their other troubles. The Cornhuskers were on a march that would take them to the first bowl game in the school's history, a game that, despite the triumphs since, lives on in the memories of Husker fans everywhere.

In 1929 the university administration was once again looking for a coach who could lead the team to glory. Dawson and Bearg were better than average, but the feeling was that there must be someone out there better than that. When one thought of greatness in college football in 1929, one thought of Knute Rockne. Approached by NU, Rockne made it clear that he wasn't about to leave South Bend, Indiana, but he did know of an excellent coach who just might be willing to direct the Cornhusker program. Following Rockne's advice, representatives from Nebraska quickly contacted Dana Xenophon Bible, who, at that time, was coaching at Texas A&M University.

Bible was ready for the move. In eleven years at A&M he had won five Southwestern Conference championships but had never received the kind of financial recognition he felt his accomplishments deserved. Nebraska was ready to offer him the prestige of a contract paying approximately $10,000 a year. Rader's Book, *American Sports*, offers a statistic to put this salary into perspective. "According to a nationwide study made in 1929 by the Carnegie Commission, full professors averaged a salary of $5,158 annually; head football coaches received an average annual salary of $6,107." As time would show, Bible was worth every penny of his above-average salary.

Bible's accomplishments in eight years include fifty victories, six league championships, four All-Americans, and thirty-five All-Conference players.

However the numbers become even more impressive when one looks at the schedule the Cornhuskers played. During Bible's tenure at Nebraska the two strongest football teams in the country, year in and year out, were the University of Pittsburgh and the University of Minnesota. Bible wanted his teams to play the best competition and play it they did.

Over Bible's eight seasons, NU played Pittsburgh eight times and Minnesota four times. No Bible-coached Nebraska squad ever managed to defeat Pittsburgh or Minnesota but they sure did try. Against Pittsburgh, Bible's 1929 squad lost 12–7, his 1930 squad managed a 0–0 tie, as did the 1932 team. In 1933 the score was in Pitt's favor 6–0, and the 1935 team lost by the same count. The Minnesota scores reflect the same type of competitiveness. The Gophers took the 1932 game 7–6, the 1935 contest finished 12–7, and the 1936 game 7–0. Considering that Bible's overall record at Nebraska was 50–15–7, if one were to subtract the Pitt and Minnesota games, his record would be an astounding 50–5–5 (Bible was 0–6–2 against Pittsburgh and 0–4 against Minnesota). Nebraska fans did not hold it against D. X. that he challenged the top teams.

"He knitted the state together behind its football forces as it had never been knitted before. He stilled the critics and he filled the stadium. He travelled the

9. D. X. Bible flanked by two of his assistants, W. H. Browne and Henry "Pa" Schulte. Courtesy of the Nebraska State Historical Society

length and breadth of Nebraska as none had done before him, not to capture individual athletes for his Cornhuskers but to capture the hearts of young and old and to build a pride in the great university down in Lincoln." Thus did James Denney describe D. X. Bible in *Go Big Red*. Players coached by Bible are quick to concur with Denney's assessment. They feel that some fans today don't remember how popular football was in the 1930s. In talking about today's fans, one Bible-coached player told me, "They [the fans] think we never had football until Devaney came. Nebraska was every bit as football crazy then as now."

Although a half-century has passed, the memories of those Bible years remain strong today. Men who played under him and fans who watched his teams can recall plays, games, and incidents as if they happened last week rather than fifty years ago. Of course, the players rank among the greatest of Nebraska's heroes. Sauer, Masterson, Francis, Richards, Rhea, Cardwell, Greenberg, Mehring, Dohrmann, Hokuf, Meier, and Scherer are all members of the Nebraska Football Hall of Fame, as is their coach, D. X. Fans still speak of the games against Pittsburgh and Minnesota and of the league championships. State pride swelled with the intersectional victories over Texas, Texas A&M, SMU, Oregon State, and Indiana. Nebraskans loved their Scarlet and Cream and packed Memorial Stadium to cheer their Huskers on to victory.

Even during the Great Depression, players were willing to overcome great odds to play for Nebraska. NU offered no football scholarships at this time and therefore every player was technically a "walk-on". Since it was the Depression, walking on could present some seemingly insurmountable obstacles. Bob Mehring, who would go on to All-Star status and membership in the Nebraska Football Hall of Fame under both Bible and his successor, "Biff" Jones, has his own story to tell about the difficulties:

When I graduated from high school [in Grand Island] in 1931, it was the height of the Depression. With both parents departed, going to UN seemed like an impossible dream. Yet, being a Cornhusker was my greatest desire.

I worked three years to save enough money to register, but ended up with only $5.00. I knew that if I stayed out another year I probably would never go to the university, so with the clothes on my back and $5.00, I went to Lincoln. While I went out for football, I slept on the grass at the State Capital. This was September 10, 1934. School started September 20.

There is no way I can express the exuberance of pride I felt when I ran on to the stadium field in a Husker uniform. I stood in the middle of the field and viewed the empty seats; my mind scanned the memory of all the previous players who had been there, and now I was here! EUREKA!

After a week, reality set in. I still didn't have the money for registration. The only answer was to go back to Grand Island and try to get a loan from businessmen I knew. All refused, but they did agree to take my case to a business club which had a student fund. The club said they would like to help, but they had a rule to only provide funds for students to finish school, not to start, only juniors and seniors were eligible. I was desperate so I asked George Cowton, Ernie Frank and others to plead my case. They did and the exception was granted.

With $40.00 I went back to Lincoln, registered, and went out for football again. I was sent to Dr. Earl Deppen for the required pre-season physical exam. Dr. Deppen said he couldn't pass me because of a bad hernia. I was devastated and desperate, so I asked the doctor to pass me so that I could make the team and get the university to take care of the necessary operation. The doctor asked me 'Do you think you can make the team?' I assured him I could and so he passed me. I made the team and during the Christmas vacation I was operated on in Lincoln General Hospital."

Wally Provost, the longtime sports writer, editor, and columnist for the *Omaha World-Herald*, once wrote of the man who became known as Nebraska's "watch charm guard": "I am increasingly convinced that no man was ever prouder to be known as a Cornhusker."

Although Mehring's experience may have been beyond the normal course of events, all the players of the period were products of the same times and, when they recount their memories, the word *tough* appears again and again. Most worked a job, or several jobs, to pay for their tuition. Some former players see this need for employment as contributing to their success on the gridiron. Performing manual labor, they feel, was more beneficial than using the weight room or participating in conditioning drills. "The weight room became a necessity because of the change in times," one Depression-era player said. "They [kids today] never dug ditches or hauled ice." Another told me, "Every guy I played with had calluses on his hands. We were in shape."

Even when the jobs didn't involve manual labor, the employment was time-consuming. Mehring worked as a waiter at the Capital Hotel from six to nine o'clock in the morning, then attended classes and football practice, and then went to work as a janitor at one of the local banks, usually returning home about eleven o'clock at night. It certainly made for a long day. Robert Benson, who was a receiver and defensive back on the 1933, 1934, and 1935 squads, worked as a waiter at the Sigma Nu house. Both of them also had more physical jobs in the summer months. Jobs such as making concrete blocks, loading and unloading freight cars, working in factories, served to toughen the body and the spirit.

One of the ironies of this situation was that Nebraska teams were so good during the 1930s that opposing teams refused to believe that the Huskers weren't being compensated in some form. Some colleges at the time did give scholarships and some made what today would be called "illegal payments."

10. Bob Mehring,
Omaha World-Herald
All-State Team, 1931.
Notice his shoes. Those
are homemade cleats.
From the Bob Mehring
Collection

Bob Mehring tells of one eastern university that made it clear that any player making the squad would be "taken care of," and that attending class was not required as long as the individual stayed on the team. The skepticism of their opponents became too much for the Huskers and several recounted how they lied and told opposing players that they were on a full ride at Nebraska just to get them off their backs!

Tough was a word to describe the times and the players, and there was a consensus among those players as to who was the toughest of the tough. When talking about the Bible years, player after player mentions Lloyd Cardwell, at times with almost a touch of awe in their voice. Ted Doyle, who played from 1935 to 1937, says that Cardwell "could hit harder standing straight up than anyone I ever saw." William Anderson, a member of the 1936–38 squads, when asked who was the best player Nebraska ever turned out, replied, "Without any doubt on my part or hesitation [it] was Lloyd Cardwell. He had the strength, speed, and stride to advance the ball wide, inside-out, and up the middle of the field better than anyone." Bob Benson describes Cardwell as the "most physical man I ever saw." Forrest Behm, a member of the 1938–41 squads, provided the most succinct description: "He was strong, fast, and fearless."

Several of the players told the same story about "Cardy." Considering the teams these Nebraska squads faced and the caliber of opponent they challenged, for one play to stand out in so many minds, so many years later, attests to the impression it created. Bob Mehring remembers the play:

"Nobody could play with Cardwell on pass defense. In fact, I remember only one pass being completed against him in his three years. It was against Iowa at Memorial Stadium and the receiver was Red Franklin. I don't know whether the coverage was mixed up or what but Franklin was in the open at about the twenty yard line at the north end, on the east side. Cardy came running across the field and hit him square, with a full head of steam, driving Franklin into the ground. Cardy jumped up but Franklin was finished. He wound up with a broken collarbone and a couple of busted ribs."

Describing it as a "totally clean play," Mehring notes that "it was the most vicious tackle I've ever seen." Mehring almost flinches as he pictures the tackle in his mind, and this has to impress one because Mehring, for years, earned money by boxing at county fairs and exhibitions. Every player involved in that game can remember the sound of the collision. Cardwell went on to prove his toughness in pro ball. He played for the Detroit Lions from 1937 to 1943 and was selected to play in the first All-Pro game.

Also on the Bible teams, although a few years ahead of Cardwell, was George Sauer. Several former players chose Sauer as the all-time greatest Husker. He certainly has the credentials to back up such a nomination. Just as

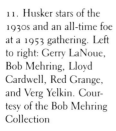

11. Husker stars of the 1930s and an all-time foe at a 1953 gathering. Left to right: Gerry LaNoue, Bob Mehring, Lloyd Cardwell, Red Grange, and Verg Yelkin. Courtesy of the Bob Mehring Collection

Cardwell has his spokesmen, Sauer was described as a "leader," one who "could do everything, both ways." One of the most remarkable aspects of Sauer's personality was his determination. Player after player described how he would be black and blue after ball games, barely able to move, and yet a few minutes earlier, he had been out on the field running and tackling as if it was the beginning of the game.

Many great players lined up alongside Cardwell and Sauer during the Bible years. Sam Francis rates mention as one of Nebraska's all-time greats. Francis was not only a fullback for Bible but he also was a shotputter and a member of the 1936 United States Olympic Team. In 1937 both Cardwell and Francis were first-round draft choices. Cardwell went to the Lions and Francis to the Philadelphia Eagles. Les McDonald, an end on the 1937 team, was a first-round draft pick of the Chicago Bears. Paul Amen, a lineman of the same period, also participated in the 1936 Olympics as a member of the United States baseball team.

Teaming up with George Sauer in Nebraska's backfield were Bernie Masterson, Clair Bishop, and Bernie Kilbourne. What made this combination exceptional was that they had all played together at Lincoln High School. In six varsity seasons, high school and college, this foursome never lost a game on its home field. At Lincoln High this group was coached by Sed Hartman, the NU player from the early twenties.

Who was the man who shaped these players? The man who turned them into football players who rank among the greatest produced by Nebraska? D. X. Bible. Following his tenure at Nebraska, Bible returned to his home state of Texas and the University of Texas. For his accomplishments at A&M, Nebraska, and Texas, Bible was eventually voted into the National Football Hall of

Fame. His players remember his coaching style. "Bible was an executive and a coach. He was always organized." He rarely spoke to the players, "but you liked him, admired him. He had control." Bob Benson draws a picture of a man who never swore, who was soft-spoken, with a drawl. The best way to describe Bible, Benson feels, would be to compare him with Coach Tom Landry of the Dallas Cowboys. Another former player stressed Bible's oratorical ability. "Bible was an excellent speaker—smooth as silk."

Bible's mind was his greatest asset. As Benson remembers, he "was one of the greatest psychologists I ever saw. I was just amazed at what he could get out of the fellows." His former players remember well one of his favorite tricks. At the beginning of practice, Bible would holler, "Let's have a team." The first eleven guys to get to where Bible was standing were the starters for at least the beginning of practice. Bob Mehring recalled this tactic with glee. As a sophomore, Mehring secured one of the starting linemen spots because of his hustle to answer Bible's call. Mehring assured me that no one daydreamed on D. X.

Bible's game preparation also sticks in the minds of his players. They describe him as organized, methodical, but flexible. He was never afraid to change strategy in the middle of a game. Bible's teams were always so well prepared that if something wasn't going well, he wouldn't be afraid to try something else or to make a substitution. As Mehring points out, Bible knew that a player could be having an off day and someone else was always ready to play. Mehring offers the opinion that "it was a slam bang game and spirit and conditioning made up for a lot."

Bible's accomplishments as a coach become more impressive when one realizes that his staff was so much smaller than today's. During his tenure at Nebraska, Bible had two paid assistants. Link Lyman coached the line and W. Harold Browne coached the ends and scouted the opposition. In addition, there were some student coaches. Bible had a rule that only seniors could speak in meetings or voice opinions or suggestions. As one player pointed out, "He [Bible] felt the seniors, by that time, were coaches." Some players like to think that the fewer number of coaches was an asset because it fostered greater communication between players and coaches and allowed the coaches to become more familiar with the abilities of each player. However, some others would disagree. Bob Benson commented, "I always wished that I could get more coaching. I think now about my speed and such and think I could have been more." Not enough practice time existed for the individualized attention and detail work that today's players find so commonplace.

Link Lyman was a legend at the university. He had been a player for the Scarlet and Cream, had gone on to play professional football with the Chicago Bears, and then had returned as a coach. He was immensely popular and an excellent coach. Bob Benson describes him as a "great communicator." One could sense Bob Mehring's tremendous enthusiasm as he remembered Link:

"At 276 pounds, he was a superman. He had speed to burn and knew all the techniques. A leader that loved to play football. Players loved him and he could coach. He would cry. He could get you way up to the ceiling. I never saw a guy so sincere."

Bible had a plan that he hoped would revolutionize football at Nebraska. His goal was to place Nebraska grads, familiar with his system, in coaching positions throughout the state. They would then teach football the "Bible" way to their students and when those players matriculated to the university they would already be familiar with the system. Such a dream was possible because, at that time, physical education majors had to play on the B squad of the football team in order to be qualified to coach. These B squad members may not have been the most outstanding athletes but they would be the ones to influence the next generation of players. The dream was never realized because of Bible's departure from Nebraska.

The 1936 season was Bible's last at Nebraska. In a career move that garnered national headlines, he was induced by the University of Texas to come to Austin to coach the Longhorns. Bob Mehring's memory of the move is so clear that the details still stand out in his mind. The financial aspects of the move generated a great uproar. At that time, Bible was making $10,000 a year at NU and this made him the third highest paid coach in college football. Lou Little, at Columbia, was making $17,500 and the coach of Southern Cal was earning

12. Two 1935 Cornhusker scoring threats, Gerry LaNoue and Sam Francis. Teammates recall LaNoue as being the "Johnny Rodgers" of his day. Courtesy of the University of Nebraska Archives

in the mid-teens. According to Mehring, Knute Rockne had made "only" $7,500 a year.

Bible conducted negotiations with Texas and then had the best lawyer he could find read over the contract and make sure it was airtight. Once that was done, he accepted the offer and made the announcement. Mehring remembers asking D. X. why he didn't negotiate with Nebraska, using the Texas offer as a bargaining chip. Bible told him that no man should ever willingly place himself in a situation where men were bidding on his services. Once he made it known that he was for sale, he would lose the respect of all those who might employ him. D. X. was a man of honor.

The state of Nebraska, meanwhile, was in an uproar. Bible had created a powerhouse football team and now that fledgling dynasty appeared on the verge of ending as the shaping force was heading to the Southwest. Some critics wanted to blame Bible's greed and criticized his lack of loyalty. Some blamed the university for failing to pay Bible enough to keep him in Lincoln. Bob Benson represents this point of view. When asked if he was surprised when D. X. announced his decision, Benson said no. What surprised him was the fact that the university didn't attempt to match or beat the Texas offer. As he put it, "If that's what the going rate for a coach was, they should have paid it." Bob Mehring feels he knows why Bible accepted the offer and, if he is correct, money wasn't the sole issue. Mehring states that Bible felt he owed it to his family to accept the offer. The money was certainly a factor, but more important was the opportunity to move back to their home state of Texas.

Local newspapermen treated the whole incident as involving something larger than the issue of who would wind up coaching the Cornhuskers. Six days before Bible would officially announce his intention, Frederick Ware's column in the *World-Herald* revealed some details of the proposed agreement between Bible and the Texas Board of Regents. Ware claimed that Bible would receive a $50,000 signing bonus and a ten-year contract worth $200,000. He then went on to offer his opinion: "For any citadel of the so-called higher learning to pay such a figure seems to me dangerous to the sport of intercollegiate football. . . . I insist the thing's fabulous, preposterous and dangerous."

Three days later, on January 19, 1937, Cy Sherman, in his column "Brass Tacks" in the *Lincoln Star*, claimed to have known about the proposed terms at Texas before Ware but had withheld them because they were private information. Now that Ware had made them public he, Sherman, felt free to comment upon them. "The payment of a bonus to any coach could have but one result. It would stand as definite proof that the gridiron sport, quite as its critics persistently have claimed, is over-emphasized. No coach in football is so capable as to be worthy of a bonus. The mere offer of a bonus by interests outside the campus [a group of Texas businessmen supposedly had put up the money] is conclusive evidence that the game is being over-valued."

13. Link Lyman, Biff Jones, and W. H. Browne. Courtesy of the Nebraska State Historical Society

When D. X. made the official announcement on Thursday, January 21, some of the facts seemed to support the sportswriters' fears. Although the official announcement made no mention of a signing bonus, reporters assured their readers that there was such a payment. Bible received a ten-year contract appointing him head coach and athletic director at the University of Texas for an annual salary of $15,000 per year. This was at a time when the president of the university was making $8,000 a year and the highest paid faculty member was earning $5,000 a year. To put this into better perspective, at Nebraska Bible was making $10,000 a year and the chancellor of the University of Nebraska was earning $10,200. The Board of Regents of the University of Texas system announced plans to rectify the salary imbalance. They hoped to raise the president's salary to $20,000 and to up faculty salaries to a top of $10,000. Supporters of Bible contend that he was instrumental in persuading the Board to consider such a move.

The transition of power was smooth. Exactly a week after Bible's resignation, the university selected Major Lawrence "Biff" Jones as its next head coach.

Bible was a member of the committee selected to hire his replacement and everyone involved in the process gave D. X. credit for having recommended Jones. Although there had been some sentiment for former Husker greats Ed Weir, Guy Chamberlin, and Link Lyman, the committee officially interviewed only Jones. Biff signed a five-year contract with the university calling for an annual salary of $10,00 the first year, $11,000 the second, and $12,000 for each of the next three.

Bible remained at Nebraska until Biff was settled in and ready to take over. D. X. went so far as to leave all his papers, notes, schedules, and itineraries for Biff. All the players from the time remember how smooth the transition was. Jones even accepted a request from the incoming senior class. Since the majority of returning starters were juniors and seniors, they felt that they had an opportunity to have a good season. They asked the new coach to keep Bible's offensive and defensive formations and plays. That way they wouldn't have to be learning a new system after three years under Bible's. The Major agreed.

In speaking with players from Jones's teams, one fact about the coach was repeated again and again. The title "Major" wasn't an honorary one, or one earned and forgotten. Jones was military through and through. Al Zikmund, who played under Biff and then went on to a successful career as head coach and athletic director at Kearney State College, summed it up this way: "Biff was military all the way." It showed in his style of dress, his mannerisms, and in his coaching philosophy.

He was certainly a man with an impressive record. In previous coaching stints, he had achieved enviable records at the United States Military Academy, Louisiana State University, and the University of Oklahoma. During all these assignments he had managed to maintain his military connection. He remained an active officer and held a position on the various military science faculties at these institutions. This was another item that made his acceptance of the Nebraska position a surprise. In order to take the Nebraska post, Biff had to retire from the service. While never publicly explaining his reasons, he decided, most who knew him feel, that the money and the time were right.

His confrontations with Huey Long while coaching at LSU illustrate well the personality and commanding presence of Major Jones. The "Kingfish," Huey Long, looked on the state and everything in it as his private preserve. No element of life in the state escaped his personal attention. He took special pride and interest in the state university. Long would think nothing of appointing the band director and then removing him if he, Long, didn't like a particular half-time show. He had promised to build the university's football team into a national power. In attempting to match actions to words, Long tried to interfere with Jones's football team once too often. During the last game of the 1934 season, after the Tigers had lost the previous two games and were losing this one at halftime, matters came to a head. After Jones had accepted the Nebraska job,

Scotty Reston, an Associated Press sportswriter, told the story of what happened next.

Here's the inside on his tiff with the late Huey Long: Jones' Louisiana State team was behind during an important game and Long came in during the half-time intermission and asked Biff if he could talk to the team. Jones said there was no time. Huey pressed and Biff still refused.

As Jones went into the locker room, Long said "Well, you'd better win." When Jones came out he walked over to Long and asked, "Senator, what did you mean by that remark?"

"I meant just that," Huey replied. "Well, win, lose, or draw, I'm through after this," was Jones' comeback.

Not too many people stood up to Huey Long, but then Biff Jones wasn't like too many people.

Biff Jones had a unique style as a coach. Players remember the organization and precision with which he conducted his practices. Al Zikmund chuckled in remembering the way the practices were structured "down to the minute." Monk Meyer, who was the student manager of the team, had a wristwatch to time the segments of practice. When the seven minutes or eight minutes that Biff had allotted to a certain activity expired, Monk would blow the whistle and the players would hustle over to the next station.

Perhaps his military training or simply his basic personality offers an explanation, but, unlike Bible, Jones liked to establish a game plan, work on it exclusively in practice before the game, and then rely on it solely during the game. This could present some problems at times. One former player remembers how the squad, one week, worked on the passing game. Jones felt certain that the upcoming opponent was vulnerable to the pass and wanted the Cornhuskers to exploit this weakness. All week Jones stressed the passing game, to the exclusion of all other aspects of the offense. Game day arrived and so did rain. The field turned into a swamp and any hopes of exploiting the passing offense became choked in the mud. However, the team stuck with it and in it. They won the game, but credit for the victory went to the defense rather than to the soggy offense.

Despite his apparent rigidity, the Major could be creative when the occasion presented itself. Bob Mehring remembers a game in Jones's first year that typifies this. The Cornhuskers were playing Iowa in Lincoln. The thermometer registered well below zero and the field was frozen. School buses were driven into Memorial Stadium so that the players could sit in them and try to stay warm when they weren't in the game. The players had been summoned to the stadium very early in the morning. Jones was present, as well as some doctors and salespeople from Gold's Department Store. In preparing for the cold, Jones wanted to learn all he could about the effect the cold would have on the players.

He had the people from Gold's there to measure and fit long underwear, mittens, any type of clothing that might dull the penetrating cold.

Everything seemed to be progressing well until the players realized that the mittens and gloves prevented them from getting a solid grip on the football. Coaches and players spent a goodly amount of time trying to solve the problem before reaching a solution. Adhesive tape was used to attach thumb tacks to the tips of the players' fingers. After securing them, the players clipped back the points of the tacks so that all that remained was a minor protrusion. After putting on gloves, Mehring claims, you could slide your hand over your face without feeling any sharpness but when a football was squeezed, the pressure was enough to engage the tacks and give a good grip.

During the course of the game, the Nebraska players had no trouble handling the ball. However, in the 1930s, teams used only one game ball and the Nebraska tactic was resulting in a very scuffed-up football. The officials and the Iowa players were truly puzzled about the source of the scuffing. The gloves worked so well that once Nile Kinnick, the future Heisman Trophy winner and 1934 graduate of Omaha's Benson High School, dropped back to pass for Iowa and Bob Mehring was in pass coverage. When Kinnick threw the ball, Mehring's hand reached up and the ball stuck to it! Mehring admits it was the strangest interception of his career and, to this day, likes to remember the look on Kinnick's face as he stared at Mehring's hand.

The rules of the game were different in the 1930s and 1940s than they are today, but Jones, like any successful coach, tried to use them to his advantage. Players went both ways, playing both offense and defense. Rules permitted only limited substitutions with the reentry of a player into the game much more restricted than it is today. Jones developed a strategy that allowed him to have as fresh a team as possible on the field at all times. He used a two-platoon system where he had two complete teams and substituted them at specific intervals. The first team played the first half of each quarter and the second team finished the quarter. Former players credit this planning with giving Nebraska the edge in several contests.

Although some fans may not realize it, even then game films played an important part in the preparation for a game and the evaluation of performances. Certainly, the quality of the image wasn't as good as it is today and the technology didn't allow for close-ups, slow-motion and the like, but players and coaches spent hours in the darkened rooms trying to get an edge on the opposition. Al Zikmund remembers how Jones would conduct his film reviews of the previous contest:

We had game films and old Biff would be commenting. All he would do would be name the player who had made a mistake. He'd say "Zikker, Zikker, did you see that?" I'd answer "Yes Sir." Then he'd say "Run that back again." Once more, "Zikker, did you see that?" "Yes Sir." "Run that back again." He'd never chew on you, but after five or six times you'd get the message. The player sitting next to you would be thinking "Oh Lord, wait till he gets to my play in the third quarter."

Many things were the same under Biff as they were under D. X. Bible. Certainly the economic times hadn't gotten any better. The story of how Al Zikmund came to Nebraska was just as typical as the earlier stories about Mehring and Benson. In Zikmund's case, the responsibility for bringing him to Lincoln rests with his county agent. Zikmund had grown up on a dry land farm outside of Ord, Nebraska. Following a successful high school career that included making honorable mention All-State, he received scholarship or financial aid offers from Kearney State, Peru State, Hastings College, and the University of Wyoming. Coming from truly modest circumstances and wanting to go to college, Zikmund was ready to accept one of the offers when the county agent entered the picture. He was a Nebraska grad and approached Al's father about his son attending the university.

The county agent brought Al to Lincoln and introduced him to Biff Jones. Each was impressed with the other and Biff asked Al to attend NU. Al mentioned that he had no money and needed financial assistance. Biff assured him that he would receive help finding a job. Al matriculated at the university and was given a job with the university's grounds department shoveling fertilizer around campus. As Al recalled the job, he noted with a grimace, "It was probably natural fertilizer at that time, from the horse barns over on East campus."

After his freshman year, Al found a job that was a little more appealing. Clarence Swanson, the former great NU receiver, owned Hovland-Swanson's department store in Lincoln and hired Al as a maintenance man for the store. Zikmund would work there for the remainder of his college career. Al recalled that the only assistance he got, without working for it, was in his senior year, when Clarence Swanson told him he didn't have to work during the football season and that he would still receive his pay. However, Al would have to make up all those hours after the season ended. Al can still remember how "easy" his senior season was without those extra hours devoted to work. When the season ended, he did work off the hours for which he had been paid. He was keeping track of them and had erased better than half the debt when Swanson approached him and told him that they were square. Al protested and offered his records as proof. Nothing could change Swanson's mind and he insisted that the debt had been repaid. One can sense a real fondness as Zikmund smiles and remembers this. An interesting sidelight to the Swanson-Zikmund relationship was that Clarence Swanson's son would spend the summers while Al was in college out in Ord working on Al's father's farm. Clarence felt his son could profit by seeing how others lived.

Over the course of his five seasons in Lincoln, Jones compiled a record of

14. Starting eleven for the 1937 Cornhuskers just before victory over Minnesota, 14–9. Linemen, left to right: Elmer Dohrmann, Ted Doyle, Lowell English, Charley Brock, Bob Mehring, Fred Shirey, and John Richardson. Backs, left to right: Jack Dodd, Eldon McIlravy, John Howell, and Harris Andrews. From the Bob Mehring Collection

15. A big play in the 1937 victory over Minnesota. Jack Dodd (21) handles an interception while Charley Brock (47) and Eldon McIlravey (25) provide some interference. Courtesy of the Nebraska State Historical Society

28–14–4 for a winning percentage of .652. In 1940, his squad defeated the University of Pittsburgh 9–7 to gain the University of Nebraska's 300th football victory. While his teams did win two Big Six Conference championships and he coached four All-Americans, two games would insure that the legend of Biff Jones would live on in the collective memories of Nebraska football fans.

In the opening game of his first season, he did something Dana Xenophon Bible had never done. In fact, no Nebraska coach since Jumbo Stiehm in 1913 had accomplished the feat. He defeated Minnesota. In front of the hometown fans, Jones's charges went out and handed the Golden Gophers a 14–9 loss. To say that this was an upset would be an understatement. Some rank this as one of the greatest wins in Cornhusker history. Commentators of the time were no less impressed. The headline in the following day's *World-Herald* proclaimed: "Nebraska's Surprise Victory Over Minnesota Most Astounding Since Those Famous Games With Notre Dame 15 Years Ago." The headline ran in big bold type for two lines across the top of the sports section. John Bentley, in the *Sunday Journal and Star*, began his column on the game: "Can this be the dawn of the millennium!"

Sportswriters and fans across the country were stunned by the Nebraska victory. The same Sunday edition of the *World-Herald* ran an article under the headline "Jones Receives Congratulations." The article informed the readers:

Major Biff Jones was a boon to the telegraph companies after the Nebraska victory over Minnesota today.

The popular coach received five hundred congratulatory telegrams from coaches, friends, army officers and just plain fans scattered over the United States, Cuba, the Bahamas, South America and Europe.

Dana X. Bible, Jones' predecessor, wired: "Atta boy. Congratulations."

Jones's second accomplishment far surpassed the first. His 1940 team would become the first in Cornhusker history to play in a bowl game. And, it wasn't just any bowl, it was the Rose Bowl, the one that sports reporters and commentators are so fond of calling "the grand daddy of them all." This game is so important in Nebraska football mythology that Bob Devaney, as he has been quoted as saying numerous times, lived in the state for five or six years before he found out that Nebraska lost the game to Stanford! Greg McBride, a Lincoln sportswriter, tried to put the importance of this game into perspective. Without any attempt at hyperbole, he stated that the Rose Bowl invitation "was the greatest thing that happened to Nebraska since William Jennings Bryan ran for the presidency."

The 1940 season had been an excellent one for the Cornhuskers. After a last-minute, opening game loss to Minnesota, Biff Jones's boys had run off eight victories in a row. Not only did this mean an undefeated Big Six season, but it also included victories over Big Ten foes, Iowa and Indiana, and a 9–7 win over the Pitt Panthers at Pittsburgh. The final totals for the season show that this squad gave up only fifty-four total points in nine games. The statistics all looked impressive and confidence was high. Fan support was also strong. Home attendance for the five games of the 1940 season was 133,000.

The Rose Bowl bid was extended on December 1, 1940. The following morning, Frederick Ware had all the details for *World-Herald* readers. Tickets would be $4.40 each and the Cornhuskers could expect to realize a nice solid financial return for their participation. Ware pointed out that NU's acceptance "assured the university's athletic department of a sum between 75 thousand and 85 thousand dollars, which will mean completion of the new fieldhouse almost a year ahead of schedule."

Not necessarily overlooked in all the excitement, but certainly over-shadowed by the celebration, was the fact that Nebraska's opponent in the Rose Bowl, Stanford, was not only a very good team but also one that utilized the *T* formation, something with which Nebraska had no familiarity. The *World-Herald* should have occasioned some concern with the publication of a season wrap-up article on the day after the announcement. On December 2, the paper noted, "The Huskers closest approach to weakness throughout the nine game program [season] was at pass defense."

The champion of the Pacific Coast Conference chose its own opponent for the Rose Bowl. The *World-Herald* wanted to know why Stanford had chosen Nebraska and sent Greg McBride to San Francisco to find the answer. In a report from that city, on December 4, McBride offered five reasons for the extension of the invitation. Reasons three through five dealt with financial matters and football ability, but the first two were sources of pride for Nebraskans. Reason one: "Stanford believes in the high educational standards Nebraska is striving to uphold in spite of tax reductions by the state unicameral." Reason two: "Nebraska's policy of non-subsidization of its athletes and strict ban on proselytizing is in line with Stanford's ethics. The Cardinals heard Husker teams are largely manned by home grown boys."

Herb Michelson and Dave Newhouse in their book *Rose Bowl Football Since 1902* have a more practical, although no less complimentary, explanation: "Actually, Stanford was a shoo-in from the Pacific Coast Conference. Finding an opponent was more difficult. The Big Nine didn't allow post-season competition at that time, so neither Minnesota nor Michigan . . . were available. Nebraska won the Big Six championship with an 8–1 record. . . . The Cornhuskers destroyed everything in their path after [the opening game loss to Minnesota]. Nebraska had a colorful coach in Major Biff Jones and an All-America fullback in Vike Francis. And so it was decided, Stanford v. Nebraska."

As soon as the invitation was made public, Cornhusker fans began to celebrate. Sunday evening's announcement of Nebraska's acceptance included the news that the university had officially canceled all classes for the next day.

Throughout the night on Sunday and during the day on Monday, students roamed around the downtown area cheering the Huskers. They were not alone. Hundreds, if not thousands, of Lincolnites joined them in the celebration. This enthusiasm carried over into ticket sales. By Wednesday, December 4, John Selleck, the business manager, was bemoaning the fact that NU's entire complement of tickets was sold out and that he would have to return hundreds of dollars to those unable to secure the precious pieces of cardboard.

Fans weren't the only ones interested in the Cornhuskers' trip to the West Coast. Even in 1941, bowl games were big business. On December 3, the *World-Herald* informed its readers that "a battery of railroad and airline representatives stormed the athletic offices early while Los Angeles hotel men bombarded Jones with telegrams and phone calls seeking designation as Cornhusker headquarters." Then as now, Nebraska weather doesn't always provide the best conditions for conducting prebowl practices. The Major decided to take the Cornhuskers on the road to a warmer climate in order to prepare for the Rose Bowl. Again, promoters from various cities, including Las Vegas, besieged him with offers to provide lodging, hospitality, entertainment, and training facilities for the Nebraska squad.

Finally, on Friday, December 6, all the speculation and solicitation over travel arrangements ended. The athletic offices announced that the squad would travel by train to Phoenix, Arizona, where it would conduct two-a-day

16. The 1940 Cornhuskers—Nebraska's first bowl team. Courtesy of the Nebraska State Historical Society

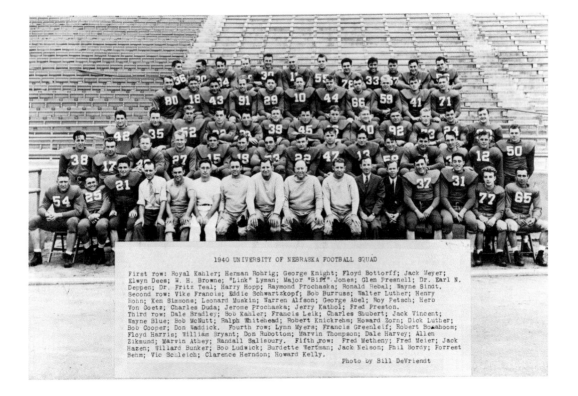

1940 UNIVERSITY OF NEBRASKA FOOTBALL SQUAD

First row: Royal Kahler; Herman Rohrig; George Knight; Floyd Bottorff; Jack Meyer; Elwyn Dees; W. H. Browne; "Link" Lyman; Major "Biff" Jones; Glen Presnell; Dr. Earl N. Deppen; Dr. Fritz Teal; Harry Hopp; Raymond Prochaska; Ronald Hebal; Wayne Sindt. Second row: Vike Francis; Eddie Schwartzkopf; Bob Burruss; Walter Luther; Henry Rohn; Ken Simmons; Leonard Muskin; Warren Alfson; George Abel; Roy Petsch; Herb Von Goetz; Charles Duda; Jerome Prochaska; Jerry Kathol; Fred Preston. Third row: Dale Bradley; Bob Kahler; Francis Lelk; Charles Shubert; Jack Vincent; Wayne Blue; Bob McNutt; Ralph Whitehead; Robert Knickrehm; Howard Zorn; Dick Luther; Bob Cooper; Don Waddick. Fourth row: Lynn Myers; Francis Greenleif; Robert Bomahoom; Floyd Harris; William Bryant; Don Rubottom; Marvin Thompson; Dale Harvey; Allen Zikmund; Marvin Athey; Randall Salisoury. Fifth row: Fred Metheny; Fred Meier; Jack Hazen; Willard Bunker; Boo Ludwick; Burdette Wertman; Jack Nelson; Phil Bordy; Forrest Behm; Vic Schleich; Clarence Herndon; Howard Kelly.

Photo by Bill DeVriendt

practices before moving on to Pasadena. The departure date for the team was December 19. The papers also announced that another bowl-bound team would be practicing in Phoenix. The Tempe Teachers were conducting their preparations for a Sun Bowl matchup with the men from Western Reserve.

On December 12, the NU Alumni Club of Southern California announced its plans for "the largest alumni gathering ever held by any school on the west coast, excluding those of coast institutions." The festivities were scheduled for New Year's night, after the game, and would include a banquet. The tickets were priced at three dollars apiece, but the *Omaha World-Herald* noted, "Literature plugging the affair promises the presence of Hollywood stars and nationally known coaches and sports writers." Others were also making preparations. The following day's *World-Herald*, in attempting to describe the enthusiasm on the West Coast for the game, almost breathlessly informed its readers that "scalpers were asking $10 for the ducats grabbed in the public sale. Those seats were behind the goal posts."

The players and coaches were getting ready too. Forty players were to make the trip to the Rose Bowl. The linemen averaged 194 pounds a man and the backfield 190. This made it a good-sized team for its day. The fact that the Huskers were facing the *T* formation for the first time occasioned some trepidation on the part of Husker fans, but again the *World-Herald* had assurances.

On December 3, the following article appeared:

Nebraska hasn't formally scouted Stanford. Assistant Coach Adolph Lewandowski saw Saturday's game with California's Bears, but he sat in the stands, where it would be difficult to attend to the note taking business. . . .

Major Jones' way of getting a line on Stanford reflects his constant attention to every angle. He will get a line on Stanford via the Chicago Bears.

Saturday night Coaches W. Harold Browne and Link Lyman went to Chicago. Brownie took along a movie camera. Both carried all the equipment necessary for diagramming. The job was mostly a review for the big line coach who was the Bear's greatest of all pro tackles for many years.

Monday morning the Husker scouts returned, with grins, notes and films.

Stanford, of course, has probably revised the Bear's T formation stuff which Clark Shaughnessy studied so closely on autumn Sunday afternoons while he was coach at Chicago and Bernie Masterson, the old Husker quarterback, helped teach the Stanford boys last spring. But Lyman and Browne undoubtedly captured the essentials.

While the coaches were acquainting themselves with the intricacies of Stanford's offensive sets, the players went about their business of taking final exams and rehabilitating injuries. In evaluating the injury situation, one reporter on December 6 wrote that he had been on campus the previous day and had visited with some players. "Harry Hopp, who suffered a shoulder injury in the final game against Kansas State, was working out on the basket ball court, apparently rounding into shape rapidly." Imagine the reporter talking to the same player today. The player would have been in the trainer's room or the weight room. Times were a lot simpler then.

On December 19, the football team, officially forty-three strong, coaches, family members, university administrators, and sportswriters left Lincoln on a Rock Island Line train. The fans back home never lacked for information on the condition of the players and the details of the trip. The contingent of writers filed daily reports. Frederick Ware's column on December 21 is typical of the prose. Datelined "On the Cornhusker Special, En Route to Phoenix," the column offered the following tidbits:

Twice during Friday the Bowl-bound Nebraskans interrupted their journey toward the training grounds to stretch their legs and further their education by observation.

Early in the afternoon 43 squad members heel-and-toed for a half an hour through the streets of Tucumcari, N.M. The coaches set the pace, and such hanger-ons as your correspondent was almost literally hanging on as the hikers returned to the station where the Rock Island responsibility ended and the Southern Pacific began.

Early in the evening a pause at El Paso put the party south of the border for a couple of hours of entertaining and illuminating rubbernecking in Juarez. . . .

Meanwhile, Ware's colleague, Greg McBride, was scouting ahead of the official party, letting his readers know what to expect in Phoenix. He was particularly overcome by the Camelback Inn, where the players would be staying. In a December 21 article entitled "Husker Headquarters a Desert Paradise," McBride wrote:

I was out to the inn Friday afternoon and I'm certain the Cornhuskers' eyes will pop at the splendid layout.

A 25-acre setting of green lawns, flowers, orange trees, date palms and cactus gardens make it a desert paradise. The athletes, in pairs, will occupy outdoor bungalows. Business Manager John K. Selleck's budget may groan as rates are $12 per day and up.

Forty-five years later, one player on that 1941 squad put it more succinctly, but no less eloquently, "The place was posh, posh."

After the Huskers arrived in Phoenix, the serious business of two-a-day practices didn't interfere with some entertainment hosted by the local community. Although Ware, McBride, and others noted that buses were wearing out a rut between the inn and the practice field, the players did manage to eat some fine foods and take in a rodeo. As late as December 28, the squad was still holding full-contact scrimmages and the practices stretched out to better than five hours a day. Every commentator assured the fans that the squad was ready. If you weren't one for the printed word, Lyle Bremser was along with a nightly live radio broadcast in which his interviews with players sounded the same positive note.

Finally, game day arrived. The players, the fans, and the sports writers were ready. Frederick Ware's front-page column on New Year's morning was especially flowery. He began by cautioning his readers that

never before has a Nebraska team played for such a high stake. The stake is reputation—Nebraska's and the entire middle border's. The Cornhuskers' will bear a responsibility borne by few of the 25 other squads that have traveled here since the contest became an annual in 1916. The Cornhuskers must show almost all the rest of the nation save their own Nebraska, and this free and friendly California that has indorsed [sic] Stanford's preferment as it has indorsed [sic] few others.

Ware described the Cornhuskers as "these true sons of the midland prairies" and then went on to exhort them to "meet the Stanford challenge. Nebraska's boys must meet it by playing valiantly and doggedly and alertly, if not victoriously, in order to demonstrate the vigor and rugged worth of the plainsland game whose prestige is in their keeping." That's quite a heavy load for any group of young men to bear. Some were more than happy when kickoff finally arrived and all the hoopla was behind them.

The game started well for the Cornhuskers. After receiving the opening kickoff, they marched down the field with fullback Vike Francis taking the snaps from center in the single wing formation, and pushed across a score. Before the Stanford fans had settled in their seats their boys were down 7–0. Michelson and Newhouse record an amusing story about that opening drive. It seems that Frankie Albert, the Stanford quarterback, could hear loud cheering from the ninety thousand crammed into the Rose Bowl. He kept thinking, "Damn, this is a pro-Nebraska crowd!" Albert recalled:

What happened was that a lot of the Stanford fans with all the partying on New Year's Eve, came to the game late. We wore red jerseys most of the season, but were wearing white for this game. Nebraska's colors also were red and white, and they were wearing the red jerseys. Well, Nebraska scores—boom, boom—and the Stanford fans see the red jerseys, so they start screaming like crazy. Heck our fans didn't know the T-formation from the single wing."

After recounting the above anecdote, the authors comment, "The remainder of the game proved that Nebraska was having the same problem." This was no overstatement. Some attributed the loss to Stanford's team speed. Al Zikmund, a sophomore at the time, was the fastest Husker player. In the second quarter he recovered a Frankie Albert fumble and on the next play caught a thirty-three-yard scoring pass from Herm Rohrig. Shortly after this play Zikmund fractured his shinbone and was done for the game. The *Omaha World-Herald* saw this as the key. "Thus was lost to Nebraska the speed that might have won, the margin of hurry that Zikmund perhaps could have provided."

When questioned about the game, Zikmund remembered the outcome as being determined by different circumstances. In his mind, Stanford was no faster than Nebraska. Simply put, Nebraska had no idea where the Stanford players were going. Zikmund feels that Nebraska was thoroughly confused by the *T* formation. In looking back on the game, after his many years as a coach, Zikmund can't believe some of the defenses Nebraska attempted to use. "Do you know that when they sent a back in motion, we pulled a guard from the line to go with him?" The team and coaches had worked hard in preparing for the game, but the total unfamiliarity with the formation made the difference. When the dust had settled, Nebraska was on the short end of a 21–13 score. Stanford had gained 345 total yards to the Cornhuskers' 153.

Stanford may have won, but Nebraska's players weren't losers. They had represented their state well, and the state remembered them for it. As Bob Devaney points out, many Nebraskans to this day can remember the names of the players on the 1941 squad. Team members are still recognized for their accomplishments. The game closed out a decade of achievement for Nebraska football. It helped to give pride to a weary, economically devastated state. The giving of happiness in such a period is indeed praiseworthy; the problem was that it set expectations for the future that would be very difficult to meet. Fourteen years would pass before another Cornhusker eleven traveled to a bowl game and almost twenty-two years before Nebraska would emerge victorious in bowl competition. The next two decades would prove to be long ones for the Husker faithful.

17. The Huskers' loss in the 1941 Rose Bowl didn't dampen the love affair with the fans, as the crowd that turned out to welcome home the team demonstrated. Courtesy of the University of Nebraska Archives

Chapter Three

The Bad Times

Beginning in 1941 and continuing for the next two decades, Nebraska football differed dramatically from what its fans had come to appreciate in the previous two decades. Victories did not come easily and did not come in bunches the way they had in the preceding years. Individual accomplishment was the only bright spot in the period. The names of some of those players remain carved in the turf of Memorial Stadium. In the second decade, the Cornhuskers went to a bowl, but as one player from the late 1930's said about the postwar period, "I was embarrassed. I didn't want people to know that I had played for Nebraska."

The "season after" started with no hint of what was to come. The 1941 squad opened with shutout league victories over Iowa State and Kansas, and then the unthinkable happened. The team lost two in a row, and then a third, and a fourth and even a fifth. Five games in a row! Two were shutouts and the team scored seven points or less in two others! The game that started the streak, a 21–13 loss at home to Indiana, also marked another negative statistic. Nebraska had recorded the 100th loss in its football history. Of course, as the *NU Press Guide* is justifiably quick to point out, Nebraska was in its 52nd season of football by this time and its overall record was 304–100–31. The season finally ended with victories over Iowa and Oklahoma, but each was by only a point and gave no evidence of anything that would signal hope for the future. Little did they know or suspect that this 4–5 record would be the best they would see for the remainder of the decade.

The disbelief of the fans and the shortcomings of the season were all pushed to the background on December 7, 1941. The Japanese attack on Pearl Harbor overshadowed the mundane cares of football. Millions of American lives were changed by the events of that day and those of many Nebraskans among them. Men and boys went off to war, many never to return. Players ended careers prematurely. Some promising prospects never attended NU and others found their circumstances so drastically altered that football became a very minor priority.

One man who felt the impact of the war very quickly was Biff Jones. The

"Major" was recalled to active duty. Like all men who entered the armed forces during the war, Biff received assurances that his job would be waiting for him when he returned. Although that promise would be kept, Biff left with some clouds hanging over him. After all, he had just finished a losing season. In addition, his personality was such that many people were not sorry to see the last of him. His abrasiveness was an irritation that could be tolerated in a Rose Bowl coach but one that could cause a lack of enthusiasm for a losing coach. Finally, many players mention his lack of rapport with Link Lyman, who was one of the most popular of all the Huskers and a real favorite of the local business community. The university did live up to its obligations after the war. It offered Biff a one-year contract, not as football coach but only as athletic director. However, he knew he really wasn't wanted and refused the offer. Thus ended the "Biff Jones Era" at Nebraska.

Link Lyman wasn't appointed head coach to replace Jones, but another assistant was. Glenn Presnell, who had starred for the Huskers in the mid-1920s and who had then gone on to a pro career with the Ironton Tanks, Portsmouth Spartans, and Detroit Lions, was the administration's choice. Presnell had solid qualifications for the post. In addition to his pro experience and Nebraska connection as a player, he had been backfield coach at both the University of Kansas and the University of Nebraska. During his one year as mentor to the Huskers, the war was already beginning to take its toll on the squad. Presnell's team went 3–7 and in five of the losses it failed to score a point. After the season, Presnell went off to the service.

Presnell's record shouldn't be blamed on poor coaching. His career after the war offers proof of his abilities. Following World War II, he went to Eastern Kentucky University and enjoyed a successful 16-year tenure as head football coach before moving up to athletic director in 1963. After he retired from Eastern Kentucky in 1972, Presnell felt that he could look back on his career with satisfaction and pride.

New powers emerged in college football during the war. Some of the strong got stronger, but newcomers also appeared. Nebraska's program, however, suffered a significant downturn. One simple explanation for Nebraska's lack of success is that the university did not have a naval or preflight training program on campus. John McCallum notes this when he offers the opinion that "whereas other campuses had naval training programs that provided them with a steady flow of healthy athletes, Nebraska had none. It began to lose and when the war ended the losing was hard to shed." David Israel confirms this scarcity of players in his description of the 1943 team as "a rag-tag collection. There were fifteen fuzzy cheeked boys too young to register for the draft. There were eleven other young men too infirm to qualify for the military, which was then in desperate need of bodies; and there were seven healthy guys nervously awaiting the moment they would get their greetings."

World War II caused not only a shortage of players but also reduced the number of men available to manage major college football programs. Individuals had to do what they could and sometimes this involved taking on more burdens than seemed possible to handle. The man who replaced Glenn Presnell was faced with just such a challenge. His name was Adolph J. Lewandowski and his was no simple task. Again, it is difficult to fault the credentials of the man. Lewandowski had experience as an assistant on the college level and was well liked by the players. Over two seasons, however, his record was 4–12. One explanation was, of course, the quality of players and the quality of the opposition. Another possible reason could be that Lewandowski was simply spread too thin. He not only served as head football coach but also as head basketball coach, athletic department business manager, and acting athletic director. One can only suspect that he felt tremendously relieved in 1945 when he was able to resign all his titles and become head of ticket sales for the athletic department.

Talking with fans today, many realize that the Cornhusker teams of the 1940s and 1950s were not winners, but few remember how truly poor the teams were or how the fans at the time reacted. These two decades mark the only ones in the proud history of Nebraska football during which the team had a less than .600 winning percentage. For the period 1940–49 the Cornhuskers' record was 34–57–0 for a .374 mark. Subtract the Rose Bowl squad's 8–2 mark and the record drops to 26–55–0 or .321. In the 1950s the record doesn't pick up all that much. Nebraska teams compiled a winning percentage of .405 based on a 39–58–3 record. Aside from the period of 1890 to 1899, when the university elevens compiled a .611 winning percentage, every other decade has seen the Huskers win at least 70 percent of their games. The fans also recognized the quality of play. After drawing 133,000 for five home games in 1940, Nebraska's home attendance for four games in 1944 was 16,161. Although wartime travel restrictions, other preoccupations, and one less game could explain some dip in attendance, a drop such as this had some relationship to the team's performance.

After Adolph Lewandowski hung up his many hats to concentrate on ticket sales, a man whose name is the answer to a couple of trivia questions about NU football took charge of the program. George "Potsy" Clark is the only man to coach the Cornhuskers on two separate occasions (1945 and 1948). He is also the creator of the famous "Platte River Spread," an offensive formation that, for many, epitomizes the level of futility exhibited by his teams. In his two seasons, Potsy's teams managed to win six games while losing thirteen. Potsy hadn't been hired simply because he was there. David Israel notes, "He had coached well and successfully, until he came to Lincoln." Potsy Clark coached at Kansas, Michigan State, Illinois, Minnesota, and Butler over the course of his career and compiled an overall record of 90–38–4.

Anticipation was great for the 1946 season. The war had ended, the boys were home, and the return of one "boy," in particular, was going to make all the difference in the world for Husker football. Nebraska's new coach that season was none other than Bernie Masterson, who had starred at Lincoln High, lettered for three seasons, and gained All–Big Six status for the Cornhuskers and then had gone on to an All-Pro career with the Chicago Bears. More important, he had been the one credited with coaching the Stanford backfield in the intricacies of the *T* formation that had proved so devastating on New Year's Day, 1941. The Husker fans were more than ready for a return to glory. Bernie signed a five-year $50,000 contract to become both head football coach and athletic director.

Two seasons later, Masterson became the first Nebraska coach to have his unexpired contract bought out by the university. Dreams of glory are often hard to fulfill, but Masterson's record tumbled in the opposite direction. His first season went 3–6 with the only wins coming over the two Kansas schools and Iowa State. The fans expressed their displeasure but also appeared willing to recognize that Masterson needed time to turn the program around. Complaints turned to "Wait 'til next year." Next year the Huskers went 2–7 with both wins coming on the road. For the first time in its football history, Nebraska lost every home game. (In 1895 the team lost its only true home game in Lincoln, but won two "home" games played in Omaha.)

Why did Masterson, who had been a brilliant quarterback and a successful assistant coach, fail so miserably? Some, including Masterson, felt that he had not been given enough time to turn the program around. Others felt that he simply hadn't had enough experience to become a head coach. One former player who was close to the situation felt that "there was too much pressure from the boys on O Street and the administration caved in." There may be some validity to this last point because the money to buy out Masterson's contract came from private rather than university sources.

By November 1947 the fans had found allies in the press to join in a communion of condemnation for Masterson's teams. On November 2, following a 47–6 thrashing by Missouri, the *Omaha World-Herald* ran a banner headline: "Inept Defense Matches Poor Offense". In the game account, sportswriter Floyd Olds described the Cornhuskers as "woefully inadequate" and castigated "the utter futility of the Nebraska attack." The same paper almost gasped with relief at the end of the season. On November 30, following the season's concluding loss to Oregon State 27–6, it announced, "Dismal Slate Ends Without Home Victory."

A noteworthy sidelight is that the paper's interest in football didn't wane as a result of Nebraska's poor season. The *World-Herald* followed the nation's college teams closely and kept an eye on all aspects of the game. With the benefit of hindsight, a warning by sports columnist Robert Phipps, contained in the November 30, 1947, edition, makes interesting reading. Commenting on the rule change allowing for unlimited substitution, Phipps foresaw disaster: "Unlimited substitution tends to ruin the fabric of the game itself, and to thwart the spectators' interest. How can you enjoy the game when you never know who is playing on your team? The result of endless tinkering with football has been to make it a coaches' game, rather than robust, legal gang warfare." One can only wonder what Mr. Phipps would think about football in the 1980s, when Nebraska has suited up and used more than a hundred players in a game.

Someone once commented that it is always easier to know what you're against than what you're for. That was the problem facing the Athletic Committee as it sought to replace Bernie Masterson. Everyone could agree that Bernie didn't get the job done. The disagreement came on the subject of who *could* do the job. Time was passing without a conclusion being reached. Nebraska needed a coach and, since no consensus could be mustered, the only solution appeared to be an interim appointee. An interim head coach is not one of the more prestigious positions in the athletic world and so the committee didn't find too many takers. In the end, the committee turned to someone reliable and noncontroversial to fill the slot.

The return of Potsy Clark was not something destined to bring Nebraska fans cheering into the street. The *World-Herald* found the appointment so unremarkable that it gave less than five column inches to the topic in its February 22 edition. Such lack of attention proved totally justified by the performance of Clark's squad in the following season. Its record of 2–8 has already been noted. The only thing that can be said in Potsy's favor is that his two wins came at home, thus gaining a small step up on Bernie Masterson.

Potsy Clark's second one-year stint completes the run of coaches for the 1940s. Bill Glassford would enter the scene the next season and carry on into the mid-1950s. When one reflects on the 1940s and the poor records of the Cornhusker squads, it should be no surprise that of the twenty-five head coaches Nebraska has had since 1890, four of the five losingest coached during this decade. Potsy Clark had a winning percentage of .316, Glenn Presnell .300, and Bernie Masterson .278. Adolph Lewandowski is the losingest coach, based on percentages, in Nebraska history. His record of .250 is matched only by that of A. E. Branch, who in his one season, 1899, managed to win two games while losing seven and tying one.

There may be a reason why Nebraska fans tend to forget how dismally the Cornhuskers performed in this period. The human mind naturally attempts to eliminate the unpleasant from its memory. Just as naturally, the pleasant tends to overshadow that which is less pleasant. Laboring under Bernie Masterson and Potsy Clark was a player whom no one ever saw and forgot. A man so tough that no one ever doubted the nickname "Train Wreck" was earned. Tom Novak was the first player in Nebraska history to have his jersey retired. He was All-Big

Seven four times and an All-American in 1949. He was a man who could so electrify a crowd with his running and hitting that one could fail to remember the score or the abilities of his teammates.

James Denney, in *Go Big Red*, claimed that Novak "was probably the most devastating tackler ever to wear the Scarlet and Cream. His glory still lives as the toughest, the meanest, the ruggedest, and yes, probably the bravest player in Nebraska history." Denney's opinion receives support from the observations of Paul Schneider. Schneider is certainly in a position to judge physical toughness. He started as head trainer for the Athletic Department in 1949 and continued well into the Devaney years. Although preferring not to choose the toughest, Schneider would allow that Novak would be a good choice. "Tom Novak was as tough as they come. He used to have a rib that would pop out of the cartilage. He'd run off the field, I'd strap it back down, and off he'd go."

Certainly, there would be those who would dispute Denney's claim. Supporters of Lloyd Cardwell would love to pit their man against Train Wreck. Most wouldn't care who won the confrontation, they would just love to be spectators at it. One former player from the 1930s who would bet on Cardwell in such a match did offer what for him would be the highest compliment: "I saw Novak play and I'll tell you he was tough. Why, he was a throwback. We would have been proud to have him playing with us." The one edge that some might give to Novak is that he performed his exploits with a weak supporting cast.

Controversy isn't something one normally associates with Nebraska football, but the man who took over the reins as head coach in 1949 certainly qualifies as a controversial figure. J. William "Bill" Glassford was from the Jock Sutherland, Pittsburgh school of football. That meant the game was played by the most physical at the most elemental level. Brawn and conditioning were the keys to success and Glassford was determined that his teams would be ready when the time came to test their mettle. This alone does not make him controversial. How he went about achieving his goals does.

First of all, Glassford believed that a successful program could not be structured around players from Nebraska. A truly competitive one had to recruit from the areas where successful programs recruited. Since Glassford associated football success with the University of Pittsburgh, that meant that Nebraska had to recruit where Pittsburgh recruited—western Pennsylvania and eastern Ohio. Again, nothing wrong with attempting a national recruiting program. However, Glassford's way meant that he simply wasn't interested in Nebraska boys. If they wanted to come to the university, they could come out for football but when it came to the awarding of scholarships that was reserved for those Glassford felt could contribute.

Recruiting and the awarding of scholarships was something new for Nebraska. As with all things new, it wasn't accepted without some resistance. With the hiring of Glassford, Potsy Clark had moved up to athletic director and he and Bill didn't see eye to eye on the subject. Potsy wasn't a big fan of recruiting, first of all because it hadn't been needed before and, secondly, because it was expensive. He couldn't understand why Glassford wouldn't use the Nebraska boys who had done so well for the Cornhuskers in the past.

Glassford's attitude toward Nebraska recruits almost cost the university one of its legends. Anyone who saw Bobby Reynolds play would agree that his talents were unlike those of almost any other college player. His election to the National Football Hall of Fame simply confirmed the fans' observations. Reynolds attended high school in Grand Island, Nebraska, which was a strike against him in Glassford's eyes. Fate, though, works in strange ways at times. One of the heroes in this tale is Bob Mehring, the star guard from the mid-1930s. Letting Bob tell the story makes it all very clear:

After the war I returned to Nebraska and went to work for an insurance company. I was travelling all week but still needed a place to live. Back in Grand Island I found this old beat up house down by the railroad yard. It wasn't much, but housing was pretty hard to come by and I got a few of my buddies together and we cleaned and white washed it so that it didn't look too bad.

Well, I would come in on a Friday and there would be a football game at the field on the other side of the tracks. If I stood on the boxcars by my house I had a ringside seat for the game. I noticed right away that there was this one player who every time he touched the ball seemed to score. I couldn't believe it, but it happened again and again.

I moved to Lincoln shortly after that season and got involved in business there. One day I was talking to Norrie Anderson, the Sports Editor of The Star, *and I told him about this kid out in Grand Island and how good he was. Norrie thought I was exaggerating. I told him to look at the kid himself and see what he thought.*

Norrie Anderson picks up the story. The following is taken from Anderson's column, "The Firing Line", appearing on October 25, 1950, after Reynolds had broken the Nebraska scoring record held by Clarence Swanson:

We knew that Bob Mehring lives and breathes football, knows as much about the sport as any gentleman afoot. We also knew that Mr. Mehring is a staunch Grand Islander and therefore apt to be a trifle prejudiced.

Anyway, we remembered the name, Bobby Reynolds. We watched for him when the Islanders swept to the state basketball championship that winter.

. . . there he was, at 14, sparkplug and quarterback of a state championship basketball team. We noticed his generalship, cool savvy, speed and smart reflexes. We itched for a glimpse of him on the gridiron.

We wanted to see the Islanders so badly—and we thought the public shared the viewpoint—that we plugged in this column that the Islander–Lincoln High game in Reynold's junior year be played in Memorial Stadium. The request was granted.

We saw what we suspected, that Mr. Mehring was not just another hometown booster. Young Reynolds was indeed the goods.

So, as we today write about Bobby breaking the all-time NU scoring record after only four games, we like to think back to four years ago.

P.S.—From now on, Mr. Mehring, we'll believe everything you say.

What Anderson didn't say was that once he had seen Reynolds in action he began to put pressure on Glassford to get him, and then keep him, interested in the kid from Grand Island. Anyone who ever saw Bobby Reynolds play can thank Bob Mehring and Norrie Anderson for helping to make it possible.

Another story involving someone closely associated with Cornhusker football further illustrates Glassford's lack of enthusiasm for Nebraska players. This high school standout was *World-Herald* "Prep Athlete of the Year," and this is how his recruitment went:

I was offered separate scholarships in football and basketball at the University of Nebraska, but my recruitment merely consisted of getting one or two letters from the football and basketball coaches, just asking me to come down for an all-sports day.

I went to see the football coach that day in his office.

"How would you like to be a Nebraska football player?" he asked without any formality.

"I'd certainly think about it."

He said, "Well, if you want to come, you've got a scholarship."

"That's nice," I said, and left.

I don't believe he ever came out to see me or even called me on the phone. I had the feeling it was sort of a take-it-or-leave-it proposition and that they weren't all that interested in me.

The player eventually decided to attend college in his hometown and follow in the footsteps of his father and grandfather at Hastings College. In case you haven't guessed yet, the player was Tom Osborne, who relates this story in his book *More Than Winning*.

When Glassford got the players he wanted, what he did with them was another bone of contention. His belief in training and conditioning led to some infamous practice sessions. His preseason camps at the Ag Station in Curtis made some think of Marine boot camp as a vacation. Paul Schneider, who claims Bill Glassford for a friend and describes him as "the most humane and dedicated person I have ever known," remembers the sessions at Camp Curtis. When asked if they were as bad as some have said, Schneider simply shakes his head saying, "You can't believe how bad they were. Some of the assistant

coaches were actually mean. If a guy passed out because of the heat, all we could do was throw ice water on him and get him back out there as soon as we could."

The head coach was a very creative individual when it came to devising ways to improve various aspects of his players' physical development. The fact that there was little correlation between these exercises and actual game performances failed to impress the coach. One example of this type of creativity was Glassford's construction of the locker room at Curtis so that it could be entered only through an obstacle course. Players became very adept at inching their way forward, hand over hand, on a rope strung from the second floor, but there never seemed to be a call for this type of talent once the season started. By 1951 the chancellor of the university recognized this and ordered Camp Curtis closed. Coach Glassford had to find another site for his preseason sessions.

Amazingly, Coach Glassford apparently never recognized the animosity his methods engendered in his players. The end result of this animosity was the first and only player rebellion in Nebraska football history. In January 1954, a group of players circulated a petition asking for the dismissal of the head coach. The interim chancellor of the university, John J. Selleck, conducted an investigation and turned the matter over to the Athletic Board and the Board of Regents.

The interesting thing about Selleck's inquiry and the meetings of the two boards is that everything was supposed to be done in secret. In fact, the board

18. With all its problems, the 1953 team could never be sure in which direction the ball would bounce. Courtesy of the University of Nebraska Archives

meetings took place downtown in the old Cornhusker Hotel rather than on campus. The conclusion of the boards was that Glassford must go. At their insistence the chancellor offered Glassford the option of resigning. Supposedly, this meeting with Selleck was the first that Glassford had known about player dissatisfaction. However, the press had heard of the petition and the meetings and so the "secret" agenda had already been well aired in public.

The Saturday, January 9, 1954, edition of the *Star* reported a "secret meeting" the previous day between members of the Athletic Board and eight team members. On Sunday the paper informed its readers that the Athletic Board and the Board of Regents had held another "secret meeting" the day before at the Cornhusker. The writer expressed some confusion over the topic of the meeting. Was it to work out details of choosing Potsy Clark's successor as athletic director or was it to deal with the rising tide of speculation over Glassford's position?

On Tuesday, January 12, sports writer Don Bryant wrote an article headlined "Petition Being Circulated In Move to Force Glassford Out." This petition, Bryant claimed, had been signed by forty-five members of the football team and called for the dismissal of Coach Glassford. However, "It was reported that the petition has not been released to the public because the Athletic Board expressed the desire that the matter be treated as if it never happened in order to avoid doing any more harm to the University's already sagging prestige."

On Wednesday, a refusal to deny rumors created some new ones. The *Star* ran a headline: "Rumor That Glassford Asked to Resign Undenied." Norrie Anderson, in the accompanying article, explained how he had asked Chancellor Selleck whether or not Glassford's resignation had been requested. Selleck answered with a "no comment," and hence the headline. Anderson made it clear that in his opinion Selleck's refusal to answer was as good as a confirmation.

The only thing keeping Glassford on the staff, Anderson speculated, was his contract. The document had been negotiated and signed following the 1950 season, Glassford's most successful, when the coach had been offered positions at three universities, including the University of Pittsburgh. The agreement was a very favorable one for Glassford. If the university wanted to get rid of him, it would have to pay him $87,500. This would cover the two years remaining on the original contract plus the five option years that were at Glassford's discretion. Unlike 1947 and the Bernie Masterson incident, the university had no private individuals waiting to help it come up with this buyout money. Anderson didn't believe that the university could afford to terminate Glassford.

Finally, on Friday, January 15, all of the details appeared in print. A front page headline in the *Star* proclaimed: "Players Blast Glassford." Underneath the headline was printed the complete text of a second petition signed by thirty-five players and made public the evening before. The petition read as follows:

We, the members of the active varsity, do as a unit make this situation public as the truth.

The actions that we have undertaken were our own doings and we were not influenced from outside partners.

It was the whole team that was behind it, not a few disgruntled players. Our stand is not that Coach Glassford is a taskmaster or a slavedriver, but that this ultimate action was a result of friction between Glassford and the players over the past years.

No one on the squad ever knew exactly how he stood with the coach and never felt free to talk to him as an individual. We would like the public to know the element of our fear.

That fear being that if a player does or says the wrong thing, he will be ridiculed, embarrassed and be faced with the threat of losing his scholarship or never having the opportunity to play again.

We do not feel that we can have a winning football team or top morale with the conditions that have existed in the past.

The team has expressed the fact that for the betterment of the university and the football team that the resignation of Head Coach Bill Glassford is a must.

In an accompanying story by Norris Anderson, the *Star* announced that it had reached Coach Glassford with news of the petition. "The *Lincoln Star* was the first to contact Glassford and your reporter read the entire statement to him along with names of the players who signed it. . . . Openly crestfallen, Glassford said wearily: 'I just don't understand it.' To this the Husker coach added a firm 'No comment.'"

With this type of controversy and strong feeling on the part of so many players, one would think that Glassford was finished. However, on Sunday, January 17, the *Star* ran another front-page headline: "Glassford Stays As Coach; Pact Officially Affirmed." At a meeting the previous day, the Athletic Board and the Board of Regents made the decision to retain Glassford. The official statement released after the meeting made no mention of the players' petition or the accompanying publicity. The closest the statement came to referring to these events was the following sentence: "The Board of Regents, the Board of Intercollegiate Athletics and the university administration sincerely hope that Coach Glassford will be able to re-establish wholesome relations with his entire squad."

Norrie Anderson had no doubt in his mind, nor did many other observers, that the key factor had been the contract held by Coach Glassford. The university could find no way to break it and, by the same token, could not raise the $87,500 necessary to buy its way out. Thus, the conclusion was inescapable. Glassford would stay. As Anderson said in summing up the events of the previous weeks, no one knew how this would affect the team or the program.

That question would not be answered until next season. One positive note was that Glassford met with his players following all the uproar and reports indicated that his personality definitely appeared changed for the better. He seemed willing to listen and willing to try to change.

So the Glassford years were turbulent ones. But was he successful? Did he accomplish the goals the university set out for him when he was hired? As someone once said, you can't argue with success, but here there is room for argument. He wasn't the worst coach Nebraska ever had, but he was far from being the best. For his seven full seasons, his record was 31–35–3 for a winning percentage of .471. When you consider that Fred Dawson and Elmer Bearg were not rehired in the 1920s after compiling winning percentages over .740 you can see how far Nebraska's football fortunes had fallen. Even Glassford's one moment of triumph, the 1955 Orange Bowl, capped a 6–5 season.

Those Glassford years do have some highlights: the sound of Train Wreck driving another opposing ball carrier into the stadium turf; the runs of Bobby Reynolds, cutting back against the grain, circling around and cutting back the other way. No one ever knew for sure where Bobby was going and he admitted that he certainly couldn't plan his runs in advance. Jerry Minnick also had an All-American season, a bright spot in the 1952 campaign in which the Huskers barely managed to win more games than they lost (5–4–1). Finally, an omen of times ahead appeared. On September 19, 1953, Nebraska played Oregon at Memorial Stadium, losing 20–12. The opponent and the score were not significant. What was, was that this game was televised nationally by NBC; the first of many NU television appearances.

The 1955 Orange Bowl is indicative of the Glassford years. This was the first bowl since the 1941 Rose Bowl, something to be savored, remembered, and yet one can sense a feeling of failure or disappointment about the whole endeavor. Perhaps the way the Huskers gained the invitation in the first place explains the fan reaction. If not, it could certainly be attributed to the way they handled the game.

Going into the final conference game of the 1954 season, the Cornhuskers had a shot at the Orange Bowl only because of the Big Seven rule that the same school could not make two consecutive Orange Bowl appearances. Oklahoma had represented the conference in the 1954 Orange Bowl and was thus ineligible. However, the Sooners were 9–0 and ranked third in the wire service polls by the time they concluded their season against the Huskers. To say that Sooner fans were upset over their ineligibility would be an understatement.

On November 13, the Huskers lost at home, 21–7, to a squad from the University of Pittsburgh. This gave them a record of 5–3 overall and 4–1 in the conference. The scenario went this way. Kansas State was playing Colorado in Boulder. If the Huskers defeated Oklahoma, Nebraska would win the conference crown and a trip to Miami. If the Cornhuskers lost to Oklahoma, they could still represent the Big Seven on New Year's Day if Colorado beat Kansas State because Nebraska would have a better league record. The Huskers had defeated Kansas State earlier in the season, 7–3. If Nebraska lost and Kansas State won, Kansas State would go to Miami.

Playing at Norman, Nebraska was a 19½ point underdog. The Cornhuskers' performance that Saturday only showed how wrong the odds makers can be. The game was never close. Sunday's *Journal-Star* carried the headline "Oklahoma Roars, 55–7—Bowl-Bound Huskers Stunned." The article continued on another page, which afforded the opportunity for an additional headline: "Sooners Effortlessly Smash Hapless Cornhusker Crew." Dick Becker attempted to put it into perspective for *Journal-Star* readers:

The Sooners of Oklahoma, a fabulous hand-picked college football corporation, roared almost unmolested to their seventh Big Seven Conference Championship here Saturday afternoon as nearly 56,000 Orange Bowl denied fans roared for more and more points.

Stunned by a final 55–7 score was the University of Nebraska, which salvaged only second place in the conference and the championship of the "Little Six"—those teams which yearly must be offered up in sacrifice to the "big red" of the oil country.

Nebraska was thus humbled on the very afternoon it clinched the New Year's Day Orange Bowl assignment, its first bowl appearance since the Rose Bowl on Jan. 1, 1941.

Blocked by conference rules from going to Miami's Orange Bowl this year, the Sooners evidently wanted to make sure that the Florida officials knew they were getting a second place club—and that they did.

Coach Bill Glassford and his charges found it very difficult to celebrate the invitation after such a humiliating defeat. Kansas State's loss to Colorado, 38–14, did little, initially, to assuage the sense of failure surrounding the worst Husker defeat ever by a Sooner squad. Coach Glassford mouthed all the right words about being proud to represent the conference on New Year's Day and how the Huskers would give it their all, but somehow it had a hollow ring to it. The only bright note was that the team had a game the following Friday night at Hawaii and so had little time to mope. After the Huskers scored at will, running up a 50–0 score in that game, the team could feel a little more optimism about the Orange Bowl date.

Perhaps the most surprising aspect of the entire Orange Bowl experience was how unenthusiastic the newspapers were about the game. Compared to coverage in 1940, that in 1954 was minimal. The papers carried no high-sounding calls to glory, no individual profiles, no day-by-day analyses of practices, strategies, and plans. The opening day's coverage is typical. On Monday, November 29, 1954, the *Lincoln Star* carried an article announcing Nebraska's

Orange Bowl opponent. The Orange Bowl had a contractual arrangement with the Atlantic Coast Conference and the members of the conference had voted the previous day to send Duke University to Miami.

In the same edition, the sports editor of the paper, Don Bryant, had an article summarizing the season. Instead of singing the glories of the Cornhuskers, he pointed out that although Nebraska finished second in the conference, its overall record was only fourth best in the league. Oklahoma finished 10–0, Colorado closed at 7–2–1, Kansas State at 7–3, and then came the Huskers at 6–4. Bryant's conclusion: "Actually, Nebraska was a pleasant surprise this year, but other clubs in the conference disappointed."

Again, throughout the month that followed, one can sense none of the anticipation, none of the excitement, that permeated the atmosphere in 1940. Coach Glassford decided that he would bring forty-five players to Miami. The odds makers established the early line of Duke by 13½. If anything typifies the apathy, it is ticket sales. Adolph Lewandowski, the former coach and now ticket manager, announced on December 15 that Nebraska had been allotted ten thousand tickets by the Orange Bowl committee. Of that number approximately seven thousand had been sold, one thousand sent to Duke, and two thousand returned to the Orange Bowl. In 1940, Business Manager Selleck had been trying to acquire more tickets for Husker fans as he traveled westward on the train.

Finally the big day arrived. Don Bryant's article on January 1, 1955, was headlined "N. U. Confident and Ready." He informed his readers that "Nebraska headquarters at the Flamingo Hotel has an air of confidence, relying on insults from the local press, the underdog role and Duke overconfidence to stir the Cornhuskers to victory. All the players are talking of nothing but winning and spirit is the thing that can determine the winner."

Sometimes even the most determined teams can fall short. Nebraska certainly did in the Orange Bowl. The next day's headlines told the story: "Duke Demolishes Nebraska 34–7." Dick Becker wrote:

In a contest not designed to stir the frenzy of either Duke or Cornhusker followers, the Blue Devils took an easy 34–7 victory as coach Bill Glassford's scarlets failed almost completely to make it a ball game.

Bowl pacts which won't allow a team to attend two years in a row were probably set back 10 years by this debacle which saw fans leaving at the start of the fourth period. A nation of television viewers was probably searching for another game long before the final play of the lethargic battle.

Becker went on to make himself even more clear. He felt that "Duke did not give the impression of being so good as Nebraska did of being so bad." This ineptitude was then catalogued. "From the very start the Huskers seemed loggy. They had little spark. Their tackling was shoddy and the blocking almost nil."

All this led to the conclusion that "this was definitely one of the worst showings of the year."

Some commentators may have felt that Becker was being too kind. On January 3, 1955, the *Star* ran a column quoting various sportswriters from around the country on their impressions of the Orange Bowl. Ralph Warner of the *Miami Daily News* felt that "Nebraska didn't belong on the Orange Bowl sod with Duke. Brutally frank, it didn't belong on any bowl sod with anybody." Jack Gallagher of the *Houston Post* referred to the events of the preceding January to make his point. "This is the same Nebraska squad that signed a petition last winter recommending the dismissal of its coach Bill Glassford. Glassford can now find at least 68,750 who'll sign a petition recommending the dismissal of his football team."

Don Bryant tried to put it all together. When he analyzed the game and the team, he found one very unpleasant conclusion inescapable. "What it boils down to is that too many players got spoiled in Hawaii and didn't like the idea of working hard here. Evidently the boys came to play—but not football." Paul Schneider doesn't buy this analysis. He feels the players worked hard preparing for the game. In fact, that was the problem. "We worked too hard. We left it on the practice field."

It is no wonder that the return of the team drew very little attention. On January 4, the *Star* ran a short article of two-and-a-half paragraphs announcing the return of the team. It stated that "only a few wives and parents" greeted the team. After describing the number of people on the charter flight, the article concluded, "After curt greetings and few smiles, the team departed by bus and cars for their homes." Thus ended Nebraska's second bowl trip.

The following season was no better in terms of victories, but a more tolerant attitude appeared to prevail. Maybe such an attitude existed because everyone suspected it would be Bill Glassford's last year. Confirmation of this feeling came on November 18, when the head coach announced that he was not going to exercise his five-year option. Cornhusker faithful from around the state felt as if a tremendous burden had been lifted from their shoulders. Even the allegation of Greg McBride in the *World-Herald* that the "O Street Gang" had something to do with Glassford's decision couldn't inspire a great degree of curiosity or indignation.

The Cornhuskers concluded the 1955 season the following Saturday, at home, against Oklahoma. Again, the winner would take the Big Seven crown. Anticipation was high, especially since this would be Coach Glassford's final game and a spurt of emotion always seems to raise a team above ordinary levels in such an event. There would not be an upset though. The following day's headlines in the *Journal-Star* said it all: "Terrifying Sooners Rip Huskers, 41–0, for Title." "Bill Glassford's Finale, Tremendous Effort Not Enough For Game N.U."

Dick Becker's account of the game demonstrates the awe with which Nebraska fans regarded Oklahoma. In reading the introductory paragraphs, one not associated with the Big Seven would be hard pressed to believe that the two teams were members of the same conference.

A terrifying animal is Oklahoma.

A vicious brute, respecting neither feelings nor physiques, granting nothing to chance and paying tribute only to its master, Bud Wilkinson.

This monster was unleashed at Memorial Stadium Saturday before 38,000 awe-struck partisans come to pay a final tribute to a departing coach and a never-say-die squad of Nebraska Cornhuskers.

Here were the Cornhuskers, fighting for the cause of Bill Glassford in his final game as head coach.

Here was as determined a bunch of Nebraska gridders as ever trod the Stadium sod.

They had spirit. They had hustle. They had stood alone and fought their way into the pinnacle of a championship game against this legendary beast from the south.

"But against the Big Red beast of Oklahoma, these Huskers were returned a tired, battered group of kids, their hearts lying on the trampled sod."

Certainly, the praise and well wishes of the sports writers that day was in sharp contrast to the criticisms of the past year. The reason could have been the departure of Glassford. People weren't carrying grudges. They were willing to let bygones be bygones and to embark on a new era. They were looking to the future, not to the past.

Now the powers-that-be decided to go after their type of coach: a man who was young, enthusiastic, bright, innovative; a man who would be all that Bill Glassford wasn't; a man who would return Nebraska to its rightful spot among the football elite. Athletic Director Bill Orwig anounced that he alone would conduct the search for Glassford's successor and that the entire process would be handled as quickly and secretly as possible.

Orwig's desire for secrecy did not prevent the newspapers from speculating about possible candidates and offering rumors to their readers. The earliest names mentioned were those of Forrest Evashevski of Iowa and former Nebraska great, George Sauer of Baylor. Both men denied they had been contacted by Nebraska. Then the name of Pete Elliott surfaced. Over the next week and a half, other names entered the rumor mill—one being that of a young coach, Ara Parseghian, of Miami University in Ohio—but Elliott's was never far from the top of the list.

On Tuesday, December 6, 1955, the announcement was made. Pete Elliott was Orwig's choice. In fact, Orwig claimed that Elliott had been his only choice and the only candidate interviewed. Elliott was the 29-year-old backfield coach at Oklahoma. Nebraska was going to the source of its torments to try to find relief. Elliott announced that he was interested and would accept the position but could not do so officially until after the Sooners' Orange Bowl date against Maryland.

Thus, the January 3, 1956, announcement was a mere formality. Elliott accepted a three-year contract calling for an annual salary of $12,000. He promised to bring the split *T* formation to the Nebraska offense and to make Nebraska a competitive, exciting team. The players, fans, regents, and state saw Elliott as the anwer to their prayers. If anything, he appeared too good to be true, and that's just what he turned out to be.

One year later, Elliott was gone. The 1956 season wasn't a bad one for Nebraska. The team finished with a 4–6 record, but the fans were happy. Elliott had shown both courage and leadership, and expectations were high. The Board of Regents, in its first meeting of 1957, granted Elliott a $2,500 raise and extended his contract through the 1959 season. The sports editor of the *Star*, Don Bryant, wrote, "The action by the university Regents demonstrates that they are keenly aware of the fine job that has been done and their rousing support of Pete Elliott is an excellent way to start the new year."

The very next day, January 8, 1957, the *Star* carried the headline "Washington Eyes Elliott". The article reported that Pete Elliott had interviewed for the vacancy at the University of Washington created by the departure of the Huskies' head coach, Darrell Royal, for the University of Texas. Don Bryant attempted to assure *Star* readers that they had nothing to fear. "When a school has a coach with a reputation Elliott has, there will always be others trying to hire him away. It's that simple."

Bryant was right about the tempters. On Wednesday Bill Orwig admitted that Elliott might leave Nebraska. He had heard that Washington had offered a $17,000 salary to Elliott. Thursday, January 10, found Orwig admitting that, while no decision had been made by Elliott, if he were to leave Nebraska Assistant Coach Bill Jennings would be appointed head coach. By Saturday, another rumor had surfaced. Speculation now had Elliott in line for the head coaching position at the University of California.

The weekend brought no formal announcements, but by Monday, January 14, Don Bryant was certain Elliott was leaving. Although he was sure, Bryant couldn't understand it. "I can't imagine who could have advised Pete to leave the Big Seven—where a second place finish is always possible and no one expects you to beat Oklahoma."

Finally, on January 16, 1957, two schools held press conferences. California appointed Pete Elliott as its head coach and Nebraska announced that Bill Jennings was moving up to take over Elliott's vacant position. Elliott signed a three-year contract calling for an annual salary of $16,000 while Jennings' contract paid $12,000 a year. Once again, the Cornhuskers were in transition.

For fans hoping for a champion, they had to wonder if stability and success would ever come to the program.

Many people speak fondly of Bill Jennings, the individual. Few speak fondly of Bill Jennings, the coach. He was a very successful assistant coach at both Oklahoma and Nebraska. After his years at Nebraska, he became an assistant coach in charge of running backs at the University of Kansas.

His head trainer, Paul Schneider, sums up Jennings' problems as well as anyone. Jennings "was a great recruiter. He simply didn't know how to use what he got." George Sullivan, an assistant to Schneider during the Jennings years, elaborates on this. Bill Jennings "was a tremendous assistant coach, but I think one of his problems was that he couldn't get his assistant coaches organized. Couldn't say you take this and you take that. He didn't show his authority as the head coach and that probably hurt Bill as much as anything." A former player offered the succinct comment that "Bill Jennings was too nice a guy to be a head coach."

Certainly his record as head coach at Nebraska attests to Jennings' lack of success in the position. In five seasons his teams went 15–34–1 for an overall percentage of .310. For those that felt things couldn't get any worse after Bill Glassford, Jennings offered evidence that anything is possible. A truly sad footnote to the story is that Jennings recognized his failings. Schneider sees Jennings as "one of the greatest guys I ever knew in my life. As soon as he got the job as head coach he started to change. He was so depressed about not being able to get the job done, it was like the sky fell on his shoulders."

To fans today, the Jennings years don't look as bleak as they did to contemporaries because of knowledge of what was to follow. Those years may have been a true low point in Husker fortunes, but on the horizon was the man on the white horse; the man who would lead the Cornhuskers from the valley of mediocrity to heights scaled by only the fortunate few.

Chapter Four

Glory Days

Two national championships, more than 140 straight home games sold out, consecutive bowl appearances through three decades, top ten rankings year after year—in January 1962 would anyone have believed such feats were possible? For Cornhusker fans, then into their third decade of frustration, such dreams were for the Notre Dames of the world. Nebraskans hoped for a competitive team, a team that won a few more games than it lost.

Bob Devaney gave them more than that. He took them where their wildest dreams were afraid to travel. He gave Nebraskans pride and identity and, most important, he did it with a smile. Nebraska not only won under Bob Devaney's leadership, it had fun doing it. Football had been fun in the 1920s and 1930s but the game was bigger now, the audiences larger, and the stakes higher. Coach Devaney recognized that and responded to the challenge. John McCallum took note of this when, in describing Nebraska football in the 1960s, he wrote that Devaney "clung to the almost obsolete belief that there was room for laughter in football." Guy Ingles recalls his days as a member of the National Championship squad, remembering that "Coach Devaney was fun to be around. He'd laugh and giggle with you a little bit." Bob Devaney wouldn't be surprised to read these comments. In his own book, *Devaney*, he stated, "That's one of the most overlooked aspects of a winning program. You have to enjoy what you're doing. You have to be serious and work hard. But you also have to have some fun. Sometimes, having fun can make you work harder."

The *Lincoln Journal* reported on January 2, 1962, that Athletic Director Tippy Dye had narrowed the list of possible replacements for Bill Jennings to three candidates: Bob Devaney of Wyoming, John Ralston of Utah State, and Ray Nagel of Utah. Given the success that all three coaches would have during their careers, it would appear that Nebraska was in a no-lose situation. What Devaney saw in Nebraska that enticed him to leave a secure position at Wyoming is something of a mystery. The attraction was certainly not in the physical plant. Devaney is quick to point out that "in some respects the facilities [at Nebraska] were the worst in the Big Eight. You didn't see much of anything that didn't need improvement." Office space was cramped, locker room facilities were poor, there were limited practice areas, and travel and transportation support was not what it should have been for a major college program. Devaney admits that "when I came here to talk about the job, I really did not inspect the facilities perhaps the way I should have." Nebraska fans can only think of what might have been when they contemplate Coach Devaney's next comment. "For a while when I got here I thought I made a mistake."

But Devaney made the decision and, with several of his assistants, left Laramie for Lincoln. There were attractions. The chancellor of the university, Clifford Hardin, was an old acquaintance. Clarence Swanson and some of the other regents impressed Devaney. These people managed to convince him that there was a strong football tradition and that support would be forthcoming for an improved program. Devaney and his associates were also impressed with the spirit of the Nebraska fans and the loyalty of high school football players in the state. They hoped to capitalize on this enthusiasm and use it to their advantage. Sometime during the next decade they must have stopped to catch their breath, but it would be hard to figure out when. Again, Coach Devaney notes: "We were so busy selling our program and ourselves in the early years that we were always either coaching, recruiting or speaking somewhere."

David Israel described the fruit of Devaney's efforts in the following manner. "What Devaney did at Nebraska is mind-numbing. It was a complete transformation. Not only in the won-lost record, but in the entire atmosphere and image of the school. Nebraska grew from an acceptable, representative major participant to an absolute powerhouse that bestrode college football like a red colossus."

Israel credits this transformation solely to the efforts of Coach Devaney:

He not only organized the team, he organized the town. He organized the state. All of Lincoln and most of Nebraska went red. Like an old tenting evangelist Devaney traveled the length of the state preaching the gospel of Americanism and Cornhusker football. He found the soil fertile and he planted among them Nebraska's Booster Club and he asked not how much you gave, only that you gave, because the kingdom of Cornhusker football was big enough for even the smallest pocketbook.

Every successful college coach has to be a salesman, has to be able to sell his program to the public, but there is more than marketing to achieving the record of success that Coach Devaney did. He was a great motivator of individuals. He recognized what individuals needed to inspire them and then provided it. Devaney has said that "good assistant coaches are the real key to the success of any head coach," and he surrounded himself with excellent people. He is quick to give credit to Jim Ross, Clete Fischer, Mike Corgan, John Melton, Carl Selmer, George Kelly, Monte Kiffin, and Warren Powers for the contributions they made in developing Nebraska's program. George Sullivan feels that "all the coaches have been treated like real human beings." This treatment has inspired a loyalty to the school and the program, and Sully feels that "the winning tradition has a lot to do with loyalty." There aren't too many schools where coaches have a legitimate shot at the national championship year after year.

Ursula Walsh, former academic counselor for the football program and no poor motivator herself, sees Devaney as being able "to find people who are willing to work themselves to death for him. Bob Devaney has this wonderful quality of making you feel like you are the central person in this world. He has the ability to give you what you need and then you better get the job done. He's not going to ask you about it." Paul Schneider unequivocally states, "There's nobody in the world that I've been around, including the military service, that could motivate people like Devaney. He knew exactly how to handle each person individually." Schneider concluded by saying, "Every man respected Devaney. They respected him to the point where they would do everything they could to help the program."

Rewards accompany success and accomplishment. Salaries are above average at Nebraska for assistant coaches. Recognition is another bonus. Assistant coaches at other institutions marvel at the fact that assistants at Nebraska are immediately recognized by the fans and are accorded some of the same adulation as head coaches elsewhere. As Frank Solich put it, "You'd be hard pressed to find a better situation for an assistant coach than the one at Nebraska." Guy Ingles, who played and coached at Nebraska before moving on to coaching positions at West Texas State and North Carolina State, has solid experience to compare and his conclusion is not at all hesitant: "You probably couldn't coach in any situation more conducive to being successful [than at Nebraska]."

Devaney's ability to motivate those who work for him is at least matched if not surpassed by his ability to motivate his players. Again, he knew how to get the most out of his players and he knew that each was an individual. Adrian Fiala has abiding memories of Coach Devaney's powers as a motivator. "Bob Devaney is probably, in many ways, one of the most unique people that I have ever known. Bob's strong suit was being able to gauge pretty quickly exactly what he needed to do, from individual to individual." Guy Ingles seconded this observation. "Devaney somehow had a way of knowing what could reach a different individual."

These observations are borne out by comments from other players. One player from the mid-1960s related incident after incident of how Coach Devaney would always be there offering encouragement, correction, or simply a pat on the back. When a second player, from the same period, was told of this attention, he responded that he was happiest when the coach never spoke to

19. Coach Devaney applying a little of his famous psychology. Courtesy of the University of Nebraska Archives

him. "When I was playing, I was scared of Bob. I'd just as soon never have him talk to me." Devaney must have recognized this because this multiple letter winner remembers the coach speaking to him "only a couple of times a season." Mike Green and Dick Davis, both running backs for the Cornhuskers in the late 1960s, each referred to Coach Devaney as a "people person."

The years and the victories didn't diminish this talent. After two national championships, players were still trying to understand how Coach Devaney did it. *Sports Illustrated* ran an article in July 1972 about some of the players who had been around during the championship years. Carl Johnson tried to explain to writer John Underwood what it was about the program that inspired its success. "He said the answer had to be Devaney but after close surveillance he had not been able to figure out what the man did, except to scare him [Johnson] to death." Pat Morell, a teammate of Carl Johnson, didn't see fear as a motivation at all. "Football at Nebraska is like pro football. Devaney treated us like men. We responded like men." After listening to stories like these, one can better appreciate the smile that crosses Adrian Fiala's face as he comments: "Yeah, yeah, he [Devaney] could get you motivated real quick."

This insight into the hearts and minds of seventeen- and eighteen-year-old boys verging on manhood carried over into Coach Devaney's recruiting practices. Like a good salesman, he knew his market and its needs. He recognized what appealed to each prospect and attempted to apply the proper approach.

Frank Solich played high school football in Cleveland, Ohio. He came from a closely knit family and his parents wanted him to stay near home to attend college. The opportunity was there to play in the Big Ten, at Northwestern, and he was approached by Notre Dame and a "great number of smaller schools." Certainly, he was not going to be a victim of Big Red Fever. What was the key? Solich's recruitment took place before the National Collegiate Athletic Association placed limits on the number of visits a coach could make to a recruit's home. According to Solich, "Coach Devaney came out a number of times." Bob Devaney recognized he had to win over Frank's parents and was willing to spend the time to do so. The results speak for themselves. Solich became an All-Big Eight fullback and is today offensive backfield coach at his alma mater. Coach Solich concluded, "My parents felt very comfortable around Coach Devaney."

Even when the prospect was a home-grown Nebraska boy, the approach couldn't always be the same. The recruitment of two Omaha players exemplifies this. Guy Ingles played high school ball at Omaha Westside. He knew he wanted to play college ball and he had been attending Nebraska games since grade school. When Coach Devaney offered him a scholarship, there was no hesitation in accepting it. As Ingles said, "The transition was logical." Mike Green played at Omaha North High School but the Big Red tradition held no attraction for him. He never attended a Nebraska game until after he enrolled at the university. Mike wanted to get away from Omaha and see a different part of the country. After making recruiting visits, Mike narrowed his final choices to Nebraska and Arizona State. What decided it for Mike? "Devaney was a pretty good salesman. My high school coach counseled me to pay attention to how much the coach doing the recruiting mentioned education. Coach Devaney stressed that getting my degree was a major priority at Nebraska. That was important. What he promised me had the most value at that time."

Adrian Fiala attended Ryan High in Omaha and for him the situation was not so simple. Adrian's father worked at Offutt Air Base and, very early on, Adrian wanted to go to the United States Air Force Academy. By his senior year he had taken all the entrance exams and had received an appointment. At the same time he began to doubt his commitment to the Academy. Pressure was maintained by the various generals stationed at the Strategic Air Command in Bellevue. Adrian remembers meeting every general at least once and some more frequently.

Ryan was a Catholic school and the priests and sisters were all urging Adrian to go to Notre Dame, which had also offered a scholarship. However, Adrian was thinking ahead. "I knew I wanted to live and work in Nebraska. My family was here in Nebraska. This was a key in making my choice." Adrian had not been a victim of Big Red Fever. He made his choice on cool logic, although "Coach Devaney was impressive."

The battle wasn't over yet, however. At that time two letter-of-intent days existed. The first was for conference letters of intent and the second, a week later, was the national letter-of-intent day. Adrian signed a conference letter with Nebraska but succumbed to pressure and agreed to make a visit to Notre Dame on the weekend between the two signing days. On Thursday, before he left, Adrian was called to the principal's office and told he had a phone call. It was Coach Devaney. Adrian still doesn't know how Devaney found out about the trip to Notre Dame, but the coach just assured him that Nebraska was still very interested in him and that he (Devaney) recognized the pressure Adrian was under. Devaney simply wanted to let him know that Nebraska was thinking of him.

This was the perfect approach to use with this potential recruit. Logically evaluating his choices and options, Adrian didn't need any high pressure sales pitch. He made the visit to Notre Dame and was suitably impressed. One can only imagine the impact of this historic and beautiful campus on a high school senior. Adrian returned home and agonized over his decision. He literally shut himself away from the world for several days before finally deciding on Nebraska. Was he ever sorry about his decision? Two decades later, Adrian Fiala has no regrets. As for Coach Devaney, "He lived up to all my expectations."

Individual after individual offers evidence that Bob Devaney could recruit both players and assistants. But getting personnel is only part of the labor. Once the players arrive on campus they must be shaped, honed, and trained into a team. Here again, Devaney excelled.

A coach's control over his practice sessions is another clue as to how well he understands his players and the game of football. Former players, coaches, and trainers all agree that Bob Devaney knew how to run a practice. The word *organization* pops up in every conversation about the keys to his successful record. Bill Jennings would keep the squad on the practice field for three and four hours at a stretch. He even scrimmaged his team on Thursday in order to find out who the toughest were for Saturday's game. The problem was that much of what a player had to offer on a Saturday had been left on Thursday's practice field.

Coach Devaney reduced practice time by over 50 percent and made sure every player knew exactly how long each segment would be. All the players had to do was consult the bulletin board to see what was scheduled for each session. Each player knew when he was supposed to be where and for how long he was supposed to be there. Player after player remarked how important it was for him to know how much he was supposed to give and for how long he had to give it. Devaney also allowed the trainers to introduce water and orange breaks after an hour of practice. Paul Schneider recalls that Devaney used to refer to them as "Country Club Breaks," but he recognized that the players came back refreshed and ready to go all out again. The lessons of successful organization remain long after the playing days are finished. Fred Duda, a quarterback in the early Devaney years, in reflecting upon the impact of those times, noted: "Coach Devaney and the way he conducted himself has influenced me probably more than any individual in my life. The way to deal with people, organize your work and workers, have fun when you are doing your job—I could go on and on."

At the practices, Devaney's willingness to surround himself with good assistants and to delegate authority became more apparent. Player after player talks about his relationship with his position coach. Receivers speak of Tom Osborne; backs fondly remember Mike Corgan. But, in Adrian Fiala's words, "Devaney was always somewhere lurking around." George Sullivan comments, "Bob had eyes in the back of his head. He was always aware of everything that was going on. He was always right down on the field. He wasn't up in a tower or a pedestal and I think the players recognized and respected that." Two stories illustrate Coach Devaney's awareness of what was happening with the players on the practice field.

Sully remembers one time when Mike Corgan was running the backs through a drill to teach them to hold on to the ball in goal line situations. Corgan had blocking dummies stacked up on a wagon and had the ball carriers diving over them. Since the players were holding on to the ball with both hands, they had no way of protecting themselves. Coach Devaney was down at the other end of the practice field, but by the time the third player went over the dummies, Devaney was there changing the drill.

Adrian Fiala's story illustrates the omnipresence of Coach Devaney and also his skills as a psychologist. Adrian was a baseball player, and one of the questions he had asked Coach Devaney while being recruited was if he would be allowed to play baseball while at Nebraska. Devaney had made him a deal. The first spring after he started for the football team he could play baseball. Adrian started his redshirt sophomore year, and when the time came that he could play baseball, he was also expected to play spring football. Adrian has horror stories of coming off the baseball diamond after having caught the first game of a doubleheader and having to change into his football gear and play in a scrimmage. After his junior season he was excused from spring football so he could concentrate on baseball, and therein lies the story.

The first day of fall camp in his senior year, Fiala checked the bulletin board and found that he was a second string linebacker. This after starting for two seasons! When he rushed out on the field and confronted his position coach, he was informed that since he had missed spring ball it wouldn't be fair to those who had participated if Adrian was on the first team. Seventeen years later, the thought of the demotion is still enough to start the smoke coming from Adrian's ears. At the time he was so mad, he took his frustrations out on the offensive players who were also his teammates. The first play from scrimmage he remembers hitting the tight end so hard that he jarred the ball loose. Both players hit the ground and rolled over. As Adrian was picking himself up, he realized that Coach Devaney was sitting right next to him in his electric cart. The coach looked at him and said, "Adrian, I don't expect you to be on the second team when the season starts." Then he drove away, leaving Adrian shaking his head and wondering how Devaney had managed to be right next to him when he hit the ground.

The victories didn't come as the result of mind games, mirrors, and smoke screens. They came as the result of hard work and preparation. The *x*'s and *o*'s on the chalkboards had to be translated into the movements of players and the reaction to certain situations. Don't for a minute think that Bob Devaney wasn't a teacher. Mike Green summed up the feelings of many of his teammates. "Of the head coaches I've known from junior high through the pros, Devaney is probably the best football mind that I've ever come into contact with. He made learning the system so easy." Guy Ingles still has a note of awe in his voice as he remembers the insight that struck him during his junior season. He was walking across campus and thinking about the upcoming game when he realized that "we were simply better coached than our opponents." He repeated this over and over again. He explained that when the actual game rolled around Nebraska players never saw anything they weren't prepared for and also found that their preparations allowed them to move the ball on the opponent. This led to confidence. It motivated the players because they knew that if they did what the coaches asked they would win.

All wasn't sweetness and light for Big Red during the Devaney years. Fans tend to forget the 1967 and 1968 seasons, but those associated with the program don't. George Sullivan remembers the four losses each season and admits that "you could see the pressure building [on Coach Devaney]". Adrian Fiala, a member of both squads recalls that the two seasons "weren't too much fun." The players recognized that "Coach Devaney was showing the pressure." Part of the reason for the record and the pressure was that the Cornhuskers were trying to change their personality. After the 1967 Sugar Bowl loss to Alabama (34–7), the coaching staff had decided that lighter, quicker ball players were needed. Nebraska had risen to fame using big strong backs and heavy solid linemen. Now the philosophy changed.

Players remember being worked harder than ever in the spring of 1967 and of 1968. Pounds were shed and quickness and agility stressed. Some also remember that the net result was a lighter team that was getting pushed around by teams it previously could manhandle. Some doubts developed. Questions were raised over whether or not the transition was necessary or successful. By 1969 the doubts were erased. The victory over Georgia in the Sun Bowl capped a 9–2 season and set the scene for the two national championships. Now observers can look back and see in this change of philosophy another tribute to Coach Devaney's abilities. It took a lot of courage to undertake such a major overhaul.

However, at the time, as one player put it, "We were all embarrassed by those seasons."

No one can deny that the overall success was there. Every Big Red fan can recite the litany of Devaney triumphs: two national championships, eight Big 8 Championships, nine bowl games (6–3), 18 All-Americans, a Heisman Trophy winner, two Outland Trophy winners, and a Lombardi Trophy recipient. His overall record of 101–20–2 for eleven seasons gives him a winning percentage of .829, ranking him third on Nebraska's all-time list, behind only "Bummy" Booth (.861) and "Jumbo" Stiehm (.913), both of whom spent many fewer years in Lincoln than did Bob Devaney. Some schools would be proud to have an entire football history that included such accomplishments, but packing such feats into an eleven-year career explains why Coach Devaney was elected to the National College Football Hall of Fame in 1981.

Despite all of Bob Devaney's accomplishments, his skill as a public speaker and motivator, and his Irish personality, an almost Rodney Dangerfield–like quality runs through the reaction of the national press to his career. *Sports Illustrated*, probably the most quoted national publication when it comes to college football, has both praised and ridiculed him.

Part of the grounds for humor and put-down stem from the perception of Nebraska that dominates the national press. In September 1968, *Sports Illustrated* picked the Cornhuskers to finish twelfth nationally. After describing that year's team, the magazine went on: "That's Nebraska, of course, and blocky, amiable Bob Devaney, his consistent coaching record and his no-nonsense approach to football are as solidly appropriate there as putting the silo next to the barn." The article goes on to describe Coach Devaney's offensive philosophy as "this plowman's philosophy of football."

Even the campus was not immune from attack. John Underwood, in his July 1972 article, attempted to describe the university's city campus:

Bigness, rather than beauty, is the mark of the University of Nebraska campus. It sprawls without rhyme through the avenues and side streets of Lincoln spreading fitfully under the duress of an ever-increasing demand on its enrollment. Its architecture is a rummage of style and shade; its epidermis a variety of brick and stone and, as a concession to modern tastes, glass and metal. An aerial view is dominated by two enormous grain silos on the north edge of town and to the west is the Memorial Football Stadium.

However, all through the period, a grudging respect for the teams the university was turning out is also evident. In 1968 the assessment was that "Devaney has achieved just what his neighbors like most—sound, down to earth success that can be measured without a lot of fancy rationalizations. The Cornhuskers of 1968 are going to be strong but rather colorless, rugged but rather predictable, effective but conservative. All of which is just the kind of football that brings Nebraskans roaring to their feet."

The fact that Devaney's teams won with strength and the running game did not detract from his accomplishments. By 1970 Dan Jenkins was putting Nebraska's coach in some pretty fast company. "A new wave of geniuses among coaches appeared in the 1960's, and they are the same men who begin the 1970's as the glamour figures—the Darrell Royals, John McKays, Frank Broyleses, Joe Paternos and Bob Devaneys. They have long since joined Bear Bryant and Woody Hayes and a few others as proven giants in the profession." To be described as a "genius" by the same author who a year later would call him a "droll sheriff" was high praise indeed, but well deserved.

Coach Devaney would probably note that the more games he won, the smarter the national media felt he became. The same *Sports Illustrated* writers who talked about his predictable offense and teams peopled with "big sod busters" were, by the early 1970s, singing the praises of his offense. In previewing the 1971 Orange Bowl, Dan Jenkins observed that "Nebraska has a more polished, dazzling attack. Nebraska plunges, reverses, and throws." In the 1971 preseason predictions, John Underwood reached the conclusion that "there is no such thing as a 'typical Devaney team.' Like most good coaches, he adjusts to the available talent."

The 1973 Orange Bowl brought the curtain down on the Devaney years. The 1972 season had been one of ups and downs for the Cornhuskers. Expectation ran high in the preseason of a record third national championship in a row. Considering how few schools win a single championship, let alone two straight ones, perhaps the expectations were unjustified. Certainly the season's opening loss at UCLA (20–17) dimmed any chance of accomplishing the dream. A late season loss at home to Oklahoma (17–14) and a midseason tie at Iowa State (23–23) erased any lingering hopes of securing the national championship.

So it was that the meeting with Notre Dame on January 1, 1973, would bring an end to an era. In reality, two eras would be ending that evening. Bob Devaney would be coaching his last game for the Cornhuskers and Johnny Rodgers would be performing in his final contest. Both men went out in style. Coach Devaney's game plan and preparation were masterful. The "Fighting Irish" appeared to have left their fight back at the Golden Dome as the Cornhuskers set an Orange Bowl record by marking their third straight New Year's Day victory in Miami. "Johnny R" showed everyone why he deserved the Heisman Trophy as he scored four touchdowns and passed for a fifth in the 40–6 win. Years later, teammate Ritch Bahe summarized Johnny Rodgers' career. "He had moves the rest of us only dream we have."

Bob Devaney laid the groundwork for his retirement with the same thoroughness and preparation that marked his coaching style. A year earlier, in

20. The Big Eight's best football coaches. As of 1986, Switzer and Osborne rank 1–2 in winning percentage among active college coaches. Photo by Dan Dulaney

January 1972, he had designated Tom Osborne as his successor and had given him the title of assistant head coach. Osborne proved himself to be worthy of the trust. This was not a rash decision. Coach Devaney had been impressed with Osborne for quite a while. "One of the good things that happened to us when we came to Nebraska was that Tom wanted to work as a graduate assistant coach while he pursued his doctorate. That was just something we walked into." As an assistant, Osborne had much to do with the change in Nebraska's offensive strategy over the preceding several years. He was young, enthusiastic, talented, and familiar with the program. Bob Devaney had chosen well, but then he had a special incentive. Since he was staying on as athletic director, he wanted to make sure the program remained in capable hands.

Starting the 1986 campaign with an overall record of 127–30–2, Tom Osborne has demonstrated over the past thirteen seasons that Bob Devaney made the right choice. His winning percentage of .805 ranks him second among active coaches, trailing only University of Oklahoma coach and Big Eight rival Barry Switzer, and places him fourth, behind Devaney, on the all-time Nebraska list. His victories are the most by any Big Red football coach. During his tenure at Nebraska, his Cornhuskers have captured or shared the conference title six times and his squads have finished in the top ten in at least one major poll every season.

Coach Osborne also matched or surpassed his predecessor by producing a Heisman Trophy winner, two individuals who garnered three Outland Trophies, and two Lombardi Award winners. Dave Rimington became the only double winner in the Outland Award's history. Together, Coaches Devaney and Osborne are the only two coaches in college football history to win one hundred games back to back at the same school. The only goal not yet attained by Tom Osborne is the national championship, and anyone who has followed his career recognizes that this goal is certainly within reach. Probably no other college team so consistently battles for the mythical crown. Year after year, Coach Osborne's charges have been in the heat of the battle.

With all the similarities in terms of accomplishments, Tom Osborne is a very different man than his predecessor. He is a more quiet, private individual. He recognizes the demands of his profession, accepting them with grace. He claims that "the interest level in the state is very high and on the one hand that's very good. It's nice to be involved in something people care about. You hate to have indifference. And yet, at other times, it can get a little burdensome, a little unrelenting. But, it's not overwhelming. It's part of the territory." All agree he makes an enviable ambassador for the Cornhusker football program, and yet he longs for the privacy and quiet time that are no longer his. Being the head coach of a nationally prominent team gives him status and recognition, but sometimes he would like to be just Tom Osborne. He regrets that people want his autograph or want to talk to him because he is head coach, not because he is a person. That makes it difficult for him to go out to dinner with his family or to appear in too many other public places. Of course, the position also increases the demands on his time. The old fishing hole, the good book, the quiet evening with his family—all become that much more difficult to find time for.

Coach Osborne also has a unique philosophy when it comes to the game of football. This view of the game developed over his years as a player and coach but a major revelation came after Nebraska's second national championship. In *More Than Winning*, Tom Osborne relates how the victory over Alabama in the 1972 Orange Bowl should have been the highlight of his career. However, he felt a vague sense of dissatisfaction, of emptiness. Then he realized that "it really isn't so much achieving the end result—the national championship and the trophies, which are all fine. But the important thing about athletics really is the process. It's the path you follow in attempting to win the championship that's important. The relationships that are formed. The effort given. The experiences you have. And when it's over, it's over." Later, he phrased it more succinctly. "The joy is in the striving, more than in arriving. I love the process—the preparation, the effort, the strategy, the players, the games. The results are somewhat anticlimactic." He expressed it a different way when asked about what keeps him in the profession. "The thing that keeps me in football is my relationship with the players."

It hasn't been necessarily easy for Osborne as head coach at Nebraska. The simple question is, "How does one replace a legend?" The response is that one can't, but that is an answer that requires maturity and time before it appears. Fans don't forget, and the accomplishments of the predecessor grow larger as time passes. Every mistake is scrutinized, every decision that proves less than successful is questioned. Other individuals in other sports have been broken by such pressures; one need only remember Gene Bartow at UCLA attempting to carry on the Wooden tradition. A tribute to Tom Osborne's character is that he has not only managed to overcome the pressure of the legend but to build one of his own.

In the 1980s, one can't talk Nebraska football without talking about the man in charge. Whether one speaks to a player, a coach, a fan, or an administrator, the inescapable conclusion is that present-day Nebraska football is the creation of Tom Osborne. It reflects his personality; it is molded in his image. The players are the kind that want to play for and learn from the man. Ursula Walsh puts it quite clearly. "We attract people who want to model themselves after the head coach." Steve Pederson, former recruiting coordinator, claims that one of the most significant factors in recruiting is Tom Osborne's reputation for fairness and honesty.

The experience of Kelly Saalfeld illustrates some of these qualities. Kelly grew up on a farm outside of Columbus, Nebraska. As a 6'2", 205-pound lineman with an undistinguished high school career under his belt he had been offered only one scholarship, to Kearney State College. He chose instead to be an unrecruited walk-on at Nebraska. A major factor was his life-long desire to play for Big Red. His mother had been an ardent Nebraska fan and the two of them would listen to the games together. "It was a regular part of our Saturdays."

Kelly said that he had always tried to set goals for himself, and he had one when he showed up on campus in the fall of 1975. "My goal was to play one minute of one game. I knew if I stuck it out for five years, they would give me that opportunity." Not the most ambitious of goals, but one that reflects a basic

trust in the fairness of the program. When told about Kelly's ambition, Ursula Walsh smiled and nodded her head, commenting that this was typical of the type of player Nebraska recruited and the kind of program run by Tom Osborne. "If you are determined, and you will give your whole life to it, you will play here."

Nebraska fans know that Kelly did more than "play one minute of one game." He ended his first varsity year (he had redshirted his sophomore year) as the starting center and would remain so for the next two seasons. Kelly finished his collegiate career as an Academic All-American, All-Big Eight center, and draft choice of the Green Bay Packers of the National Football League. Today he reflects upon the experience with pride and satisfaction.

Like Coach Devaney, Tom Osborne has good assistants, men whom he chose to put his program into operation. Kelly is quick to give credit to them. Boyd Epley helped him to build up his body. To compete on the Division I level, Saalfeld needed both bulk and strength. Following Boyd's regimens added both to his body. Kelly developed a special relationship with Milt Tenopir. "Milt was willing to work with you no matter how bad you were. Without his patience I might not have made it. He liked my work habits. He knew I would take whatever he would throw at me." Sincerity marks every word as Kelly concludes, "I love the guy dearly."

After talking with players from the Osborne years one can't help but notice the differences between Coach Osborne and Coach Devaney when it comes to coaching styles. George Sullivan is someone in a position to notice such things, and he readily admits that differences exist. "Bob was probably more of a leader in delegating authority than Tom. Tom likes to be more on top of specific things than Bob did. Tom's always about two steps ahead [of everyone else]." Bob Devaney is the first to admit this difference. "Tom is a better organizer than I am." Sully feels that Devaney was also more relaxed on the practice field. "If Bob didn't like the way it [practice] was going, he'd blow his whistle and call it off. Tom would never do that." If the style is different from Devaney's, the end result is the same. After beginning his pro career with the Green Bay Packers, Kelly Saalfeld was traded to the New York Giants. Reflecting on his professional

21. Always planning the next move. Photo by Dan Dulaney

22. Part of the "Brain Trust." Left to right: Assistant Coaches Cletus Fischer and Jack Pierce, Head Coach Tom Osborne, and Assistant Coaches Gene Huey and Frank Solich. Photo by Dan Dulaney

career, he concludes, "We'd go into games better prepared with Nebraska than we would with the Giants."

Sullivan's comments about Osborne's attention to detail are borne out by the assistant coaches. Frank Solich, the offensive backfield coach, makes it quite clear that Tom Osborne is not simply a "public relations administrator." Osborne "actually gets into the coaching. He sets the overall strategy for the games." At the same time, however, "He is very open to ideas and suggestions."

Players, too, are aware of how important the little things are to Coach Osborne. Fans are familiar with the coach's continued references to the grading of film and the ratings of players' performances. To a man concerned with the process of preparation and the execution of strategy, such mathematical precision is important. Kelly Saalfeld can laugh today about one such incident, which was no laughing matter at the time. In the first of the two 1978 meetings between Nebraska and Oklahoma, the Sooner linebackers were blitzing on the backside during running plays. The Husker game plan wasn't designed to stop this, so Kelly adjusted his blocking assignments during the course of the game. The adjustment was so successful that the Huskers ran more than forty isolation plays and fullback Andra Franklin had a big afternoon. The end result was a 17–14 Nebraska victory.

On Monday, the players received their grades on the previous Saturday's performance. Kelly remembers his grades as being the lowest of his varsity career. When he questioned the coaches he was told that he had failed to properly carry out his blocking assignments on almost every one of the isolation plays. Kelly then tried to explain what had happened and realized that his major mistake had been not informing the coaches on the sidelines of his adjustment during the game. What he was doing violated some of Coach Osborne's basic offensive rules and it didn't matter whether the adjustment had been successful. The key was that the coaches didn't know about it. Since adjustments were made in every game, Kelly recognizes that the problem wasn't the change in tactics but the fact the change was made without the knowledge of the sideline. Coach Osborne and his staff want to know everything that is happening on the field.

Fans aren't always as generous or as attentive to detail as the coaches and players. Sometimes evaluations are made that are unfair, or at least inaccurate. One of the most frequently heard criticisms of Tom Osborne is that he lacks the motivational skills of Bob Devaney. After a loss, some critic always concludes that the Huskers were uninspired or lacked motivation. A member of the Cornhusker squads from the mid-1970s would dispute such criticism. "He [Osborne] doesn't wear it out, but when he needs to he can motivate. You know when he's upset. Believe me, when he raises his voice, everybody listens."

Saalfeld has a specific example to illustrate the above comments. "I can think of one game in particular that I wish everybody in the state of Nebraska could have been there to hear the halftime talk. That was the 1977 Liberty Bowl. We were behind and the man [Osborne] lost his voice in about half a minute. So, there was some motivation in that speech." For the fans who don't remember that particular contest, Nebraska trailed North Carolina 14–7 at the half and was down 17–7 in the third quarter before two fourth-quarter Randy Garcia touchdown passes pulled out a 21–17 victory.

As noted previously, the only Devaney accomplishment unmatched by Coach Osborne is the winning of a national championship. The cliché "so near and yet so far" is an apt summary of this quest. In 1978 the Huskers were in a position to grasp the brass ring after their 17–14 victory over Oklahoma. Then the unexpected: a loss at home the following week to Missouri, 35–31, and, most unbelievable of all, an Orange Bowl date with the Oklahoma Sooners. The 31–24 New Year's Eve loss gave the Cornhuskers a season record of 9–3 and eighth place in the final national rankings.

The early 1980s witnessed the arrival on campus of the "Scoring Explosion," the group that some sportswriters liked to call "Earth, Wind, and Fryar." A critic would have a hard time coming up with a more potent backfield than the one containing Turner Gill, Mike Rozier, and Irving Fryar. The group would wind up setting all sorts of offensive records while at Nebraska. Mike Rozier became Nebraska's second Heisman Trophy winner and Irving Fryar was the top draft choice of the National Football League. With a group like this, it appeared as if Coach Osborne's time had come.

Once again, fate intervened. The 1981 squad took a little while to jell. Early season losses at Iowa (10–7) and to Penn State in Lincoln (30–24) convinced Coach Osborne to turn to his talented sophomores. This decision resulted in eight straight wins, a Big Eight championship, and a meeting with Clemson in the Orange Bowl. Normally, a 9–2 record doesn't qualify a team for consideration for the national championship, but 1981 was a strange year. No team had come out and truly taken charge of the race. By kickoff of the Orange Bowl, contenders Alabama and Georgia had been upset and it came down to Clemson and Nebraska to battle it out for the title. Given the excellent performance of Clemson and the repeated mistakes of Nebraska, one could summarize the game by saying, "Clemson did everything right and Nebraska didn't." The Tigers' 22–15 win gave them their first national title and left Big Red with a 9–3 record and a ninth place end of season ranking.

With a season of maturity under their belts the Huskers were ready for the 1982 season. The team was strong and the commitment was there. After scoring 110 points in their first two games, the Cornhuskers traveled to the Nittany Valley to take on Joe Paterno's boys. Looking back, one can sense that this was to be Paterno's year. A well-liked, honest, and able coach who had been at or near the top for two decades, he too was in search of his first national championship. Nebraska was leading in the fourth quarter until a last gasp rally gave the Nittany Lions a 27–24 victory. Television replays show a crucial call in that final drive was questionable, but the game was over and the Huskers had lost. Ten straight victories, including a 17–14 win over LSU in the Orange Bowl, weren't enough to erase the blemish from Nebraska's record. When the votes were in, Joe Paterno and his Penn State Nittany Lions had won the national championship. Tom Osborne's Cornhuskers finished third in both major polls.

The "Scoring Explosion" had one more season to perform and this time the entire state of Nebraska was confident of a national title. The season certainly seemed to be careening in that direction. Rozier ran, Gill threw, Fryar caught, and the points mounted. Minnesota fell 84–13, Syracuse 63–7. In the Big Eight the Huskers didn't let up. The Colorado Buffaloes went down 69–19, the Kansas State Wildcats 51–25, and the Iowa State Cyclones 72–29. When Big Red left Norman, Oklahoma, with a 28–21 win, Nebraska had won its third straight Big Eight crown and third consecutive invitation to the Orange Bowl. After running off twenty-two wins in a row, over two seasons, and being number one in the national polls for the entire 1983 campaign, a victory on New Year's Day would unquestionably give Tom Osborne his first national championship.

Aside from the Rose Bowl and Cotton Bowl, in certain situations, one normally doesn't think of a home field advantage in the major bowl games. In fact, because of the Big Eight's contractual relationship with the Orange Bowl, Nebraska officially was the home team on January 1, 1984. However, when the "home team" has to travel 1,700 miles and the "visiting team" is playing in its own stadium, there seems to be something askew. The University of Miami Hurricanes blocked the road to Nebraska's national championship hopes. The Hurricanes had completed a storybook season, capped by the bowl bid, but sportswriters and fans didn't see them as presenting a serious obstacle to Big Red's chances. After all, this was the Cornhuskers' year. Once again, it was not to be.

After falling behind 17–0 in the first quarter, the Huskers rallied to trail only 17–14 at the half. By the end of the third quarter the 'Canes had a 14 point lead, but remember the "Scoring Explosion." Two touchdowns in the fourth quarter, the second with less than a minute to play, brought Nebraska within an extra point of a tie and the national championship. Red Auerbach, the famed coach of the Boston Celtics, once said that "ties are like kissing your sister through a screen door." Although Tom Osborne wouldn't use such a colorful description, he would certainly agree with the sentiment. A man interested in the process of the game, the preparation, and the competition doesn't play for ties, no matter what is on the line. Nebraska went for two. Turner Gill's pass to Jeff Smith was deflected off his fingertips and, by a matter of inches, Nebraska had missed its third straight opportunity for the national title.

If one didn't know better, one would almost be willing to believe in a jinx or a

hex on Nebraska. To have come so close so often and gone away empty-handed was hard for some to take. Steve Richardson, writing in *The Sporting News'* 1984 preseason football edition, reflected on the loss. The title of the piece was "The Season After: Nebraska Remembers What Could Have Been," and it opened: "The Orange Bowl won't be forgotten here [in Nebraska] because football is more than a Saturday occurrence in this cornfield state. It is a happening that is nearly a religious experience. Big Red games are more important than milestones in life. Marriages are scheduled around home games. Births and funerals would be too, but God doesn't wear red, necessarily."

This reference to some sort of relationship between football and a divinity is a favorite approach of sportswriters. Doug Looney, writing in *Sports Illustrated* in 1975, had referred to a similar connection:

It's not as if there's nothing in the state of Nebraska except football. You can go to a museum in Lincoln and see the fossil of the world's largest elephant. Or sit on a fence and wait for a pheasant to fly up. Or go to any town and applaud the changing traffic signal, booing when it gets stuck on yellow.

Or you can do some dull things. It's up to you. What happened, for those of you that slept through this in school, is that when God went to work creating Nebraska, He thought: "OK, I keep giving other areas of this country mountains,

23. After a quarter of a century, John Melton still expects his Husker linebackers to shut down every opponent. Photo by Dan Dulaney

beaches, stuff like that. Everywhere I look, beauty. I need a change." What resulted is a landscape of wall-to-wall dust. It's the perfect environment if you're a vacuum sweeper. To try to make up, God later gave Nebraska football.

Tom Osborne knows better. He knows that despite the pressure and the hype, football is still a game played by young men striving to reach maturity, to discover more about themselves and their world. He strives mightily to keep it all in perspective. Player after player mentioned a theme that Coach Osborne stresses again and again. One player remembered the speech word for word. "You have four priorities in your life. God comes first, your family second, academics third, and football fourth."

The University of Nebraska and its fans can be proud of their football program and its leader. Tom Osborne wrote, in *More Than Winning*, "My personal philosophy of coaching is this: To make an effort to win in a manner that reflects well on the university, that promotes the personal development of the players, and that has a positive effect on young people." No one can deny that he adheres to this credo.

§2

Behind the Scenes

Chapter Five

The Training Room

When a man has won back-to-back national championships, you listen to what he has to say. "The head trainer in a program is as important as any coach, any athlete—perhaps more so." Bob Devaney feels that the head trainers he worked with at Nebraska, Paul Schneider and George Sullivan, contributed much to the success of the program. While Paul Schneider wouldn't go so far as to take credit away from the coach, his experience at Nebraska under four head coaches convinces him of the truth in Devaney's statement. "The old trainers were the ones who wiped guys off and gave them water but they weren't educated as to what the human body can do and tolerate and how long it takes to heal. By the 1950s, that had all changed. Coaches had to realize that." Schneider quickly points out that Bob Devaney was the first coach he worked under to realize the importance of the trainer and to listen to his advice.

To understand the present-day responsibilities of the trainer, there is no better place to start than with George Sullivan. After all, George is in his fourth decade as part of the trainer's staff at the university. Not too much has gone on since the early 1950s that he doesn't know about or hasn't taken part in.

Although there have been many medical advances and innovations in training philosophy since he began in 1952, George Sullivan recognizes that the role of the trainer has changed very little. According to him, the responsibilities of the head trainer are threefold. First is the prevention of injuries. He and his staff are always designing protective pads, checking fields and playing conditions, overseeing any detail that could relate to the physical well-being of the athlete. Second is the responsibility of providing emergency care and working with the team physicians. Sullivan describes this function as that of a liaison between the coaches and the doctors. Finally, the trainer is responsible for rehabilitation of injuries. He works in the area of physical therapy to insure the best possible opportunity for the recovery of the student athlete. Although the second role is the most visible and the one the fans most associate with Sullivan, he would like to think that his success with the first is the one most valued by the university.

So much for the quantifiable chores. The role of the trainer encompasses much more. Player after player has spoken of Schneider and Sullivan's activities and their importance to the program. Many of the comments refer to the trainers' talents as psychologists. Mike Green remarked, "Paul and Sully can probably qualify as psychoanalysts. They must have hundreds of stories of these behemoths closing the door of the training room and bawling their eyes out." Adrian Fiala went so far as to say, "Sometimes I think Sully is a better motivator than Devaney." This is high praise indeed from the former linebacker.

When asked about comments such as Green's and Fiala's and references to his motivational and psychological skills, Sullivan chuckled. As he lit his pipe and leaned back in his office chair, his eyes twinkling, he said, "The trainer is in a special place. The fact that he is connected with medicine gives him status. The trainer is laying the hands on the injury and a person likes that. It creates a personal bond." Interestingly enough, Adrian Fiala expressed almost the same concept when he discussed Sullivan's role. "He is one of the best physical trainers whose hands you would want laid on you." George Sullivan also has some ideas about how the players view him. He recognizes that he is somewhere between the players and the coaches. Not being a coach makes him appear more accessible. Also, there is the bond he talked about above. Combine the two and players seem to open up more to him.

Tom Osborne recognizes this role of the trainer and also the responsibility it imparts. "The trainer is in the middle ground. He's kind of an advocate for the players. The players feel he is on their side. He doesn't want them to be worked too hard, doesn't normally want them to play if they're hurt. Yet the trainer is in a difficult situation because he is part of the establishment and he doesn't want the players using him as an excuse. So, the trainer has to make some hard judgments."

Sullivan recognizes that, while each is unique, the athletes share many traits. "The player has left his mother and we become kind of mother hens to them. You get to know your kids. You know their personal feelings. Some of these kids like a good butt chewing. I've had some kids here that I pretend I'm madder than hell at and then they follow me around." Real affection resonates in George's voice as he makes those comments. One also senses the pride as he points out how many of them return to visit with him after their playing days are finished. "They never forget to come back. Seems like they always come back to the training room. They like the memories." When asked about the trainers, Mike Green said, "They are the nannies. Their personalities made practice bearable."

George has had good cooperation from the coaching staff. Referring to respect for the trainer's word, he said, "I think [on the collegiate level] it's pretty good." However, every once in a while, Sully runs into some skepticism. With a laugh, he noted, "I never had a problem of doubt [about player injuries] with head coaches. Got to admit, I've known a few assistant coaches who thought they knew somebody better to treat it [the injury]. I've caught 'em a couple of times." Again, he sucks on the pipe and his eyes twinkle as he recounts these experiences.

As with all parts of the athletic program, the training room has a number of unsung heroes. George Sullivan would be the first to admit that he couldn't do his job without the aid of his assistants. Presently, Sullivan has on his staff two physical therapists, three certified trainers (the physical therapists are also

24. "Sully" laying on the healing hands. Photo by Dan Dulaney

certified trainers), and ten student trainers. The numbers appear large until one realizes that this staff is responsible for all the athletic teams at the university, not just football. In view of this, one sometimes wonders where the coverage comes from for so many athletes.

Part of the success in providing care and attention for over five hundred athletes a year comes from organization and analysis. Tasks are broken down and assigned on a pretty specific basis. Taping players' ankles before each practice is a good example. Counting varsity, freshmen and red shirts, the training staff has to tape between four and five hundred ankles a day. Sully described the timetable. "We start taping at 12:15 and have to get them up to meetings by two o'clock. It's a real push to get them up there." The key, again, is organization. "It takes 2.2 minutes to tape an ankle."

When looking back over the last three decades, Sullivan can see some very significant changes in the football program and the support services. One of the more controversial has been the introduction of artificial turf. George doesn't agree with those who bemoan this innovation. Overall, he thinks that artificial turf "has been a plus for Nebraska. It is tackier [than grass], but not as dangerous. You don't have to worry about wounds getting dirty or the unevenness of the playing surface. I think going to this type of turf prevented a lot of injuries." Sullivan concedes that some new injuries, such as turf toe and abrasions, have developed but feels that the overall benefit outweighs the negatives. His opinion is seconded by Coach Osborne, who notes that artificial turf has made for a faster game and a little different game because of the advantage it gives to the faster, quicker player. The head coach would choose an artificial over a natural surface because "it provides a more uniform surface."

Another area of change has been one that probably the average fan never considers. This is liability insurance coverage. According to Sullivan, no one ever used to think about this item, and now "insurance costs are monumental." When he started with the program in 1952, the year's insurance premium was less than $2,000. In 1985 it was $38,000. Overall inflation plays a role in this increase, as do rising hospital costs, and the increased number of players involved in the sport. Whatever the reason, this is an item of which the head trainer must be cognizant.

Weight training is one other area of change. Under Boyd Epley, Nebraska has developed into the Mecca of weight training. George remembers when weight training didn't have the support that it does today. He can even tell you who the first Husker to lift seriously was and where the weights came from: Bob Brown and his weights were a gift. As George remembers it,

Mr. [Walt] Ferris, who owned the National Manufacturing Company, broke his arm and asked me if I would work with him to rehabilitate it. When he completed his program, he asked me if there was anything our program needed. He wanted to give me a gift to thank me for helping him out. Well, I mentioned we could use some weights. Mr. Ferris went back to his company and had them take some big steel plates and attach them to steel bars. That's where our weights came from. After Bob Brown had been drafted by the pros, he asked me if he could take the weights home over the summer to work out and get in shape. I told him it was fine as long as he made sure to return them. He promised me he would, and off he went. That was the last I saw of the weights. They're probably still in the trunk of Bob's car.

Sullivan's recollections of how the present weight program got started differ a little from Boyd's. Sullivan claims that Bob Devaney was very interested in off-season conditioning programs and had George and Cletus Fischer travel around the country visiting other schools and investigating their programs. Sullivan and Fischer came back and put together the ideas for the Huskers' program. The original weights, now in the "strength museum," were purchased from a bankrupt health club in Lincoln. Tippy Dye, the athletic director, had sent Sullivan and the athletic business manager to a "going out of business" sale to see if they could pick up any bargains for the athletic program.

Perhaps the biggest area of change has been in equipment development. Sullivan feels that all the innovation in play selection and execution, speed, size, and endurance can be tied to these changes. "Equipment changes over the last thirty years have allowed a different type of game. Protective gear allows for more emphasis on technique, timing. It's not a brawn game anymore." He cites the hard helmets and face masks as an example. The development of this protective gear allowed for a change in blocking techniques and rules governing blocking. This, in turn, allowed different offensive strategies to develop.

Without mobility, a football player wouldn't be worth too much, and here, too, the advances in equipment have been dramatic. Something as common as taping an ankle reflects this. "Thirty-five years ago you used to put a muslin wrap around the ankle and then used black friction tape." Today, the university's football program spends more than $85,000 per year on tape. If asked, Sullivan can recite exactly where such money goes. "You have 2,400 cases of elastic tape, 1,000 cases of one width of outer wrap. . . ." In 1952, the trainer used approximately ten cases of tape costing around $100.

Once the ankle is taped, the player puts on his shoes. When George started in the program, each player received one pair of shoes, "and they probably got handed down two or three times. Now, a player goes through five pair of shoes a year." When queried about the origin of these changes and the reasons for the continuing development of new products, Sullivan cites the big business that football has become. When he started, a season ticket cost approximately what a single game ticket goes for today. The conclusion is inescapable. "There's money to be spent on this type of thing. Thirty years ago there wasn't money for anything."

All these innovations have not changed the basic structure of the human body. Pre–World War II players, almost to a man, continually comment on the greater number of injuries involved in today's game. Some blame it on platooning, which allows for fresh players in the game at all times. Others see the more liberal substitution rules as allowing bigger players, three-hundred-pounders, to play for only a few plays at a time when, under the old rules, they would have had to go the whole game and wouldn't have been able to carry all that weight. Some others claim that players today, despite the conditioning programs, are simply not in as good shape as players were thirty or forty years ago.

George Sullivan disagrees with the assessment. In fact, he denies that any more injuries occur today than did thirty or forty years ago. He feels that "there were a lot more injuries thirty years ago that didn't get treated. We are just more aware of them today and we have so many more players." Most of the players he works with are not into "macho" role-playing. They recognize the necessity of being in top physical shape and are not unwilling to report injuries or illnesses. George claims that very rarely has he had a problem with players trying to hide injuries from the coaching or training staffs.

All one has to do is see George out on the field tending to an injured player to know how much he cares. To him, athletic training is more than a job. The hours can't be compensated for in dollars alone. There has to be an emotional involvement. This involvement manifests itself in the superior way he handles his responsibilities. The honors and awards he has garnered over the past three decades attest to his abilities. The greatest recognition, though, and the one Sully most cherishes, comes when former players return to the training room to say hello.

Chapter Six

Strength Training

Tom Osborne has time and time again stressed the importance of a weight-training program both for building player's bodies and as a recruiting tool. As one of the earliest supporters of a Nebraska weight-training program, he was instrumental in getting Boyd Epley off on the right foot.

As Epley remembers it, Osborne was the first Nebraska coach to recognize the benefits of weight training. Epley had come to Nebraska as a pole vaulter. After injuring his back on several occasions, he attempted to rehabilitate it through a weight-training program. An almost fairy-tale quality permeates the story.

Once upon a time, in a dark corner of the Coliseum, there was a little room and in this little room were a few pieces of equipment—a universal machine and five or six dumbbells. An unknown student athlete was working out with this equipment when a couple of football players asked him what he was doing. They had been injured and wondered if what he was doing could help them. The student athlete, whose name was Boyd Epley, said that he certainly believed it could, and so they started working out with him. Today that athlete, no longer unknown, is one of the foremost strength coaches in the world, Nebraska has the largest collegiate weight room in the world, and those few pieces of original equipment occupy a proud place in this "Strength Complex."

Sometimes a fairy tale can come true, and this time it did. When those few injured Huskers returned to practice, Tom Osborne recognized the differences in their bodies and asked what had happened. As Epley notes, "It was remarkable at the time for someone to make such progress lifting weights. In fact, the practice [of lifting] was not recommended. It was frowned upon." To follow up on this, Tom Osborne, who was still an assistant coach at the time, called Epley into his office. Boyd wasn't sure whether he was going to be praised for the results or chewed out for introducing the players to the weights.

As it turned out, both Coach Osborne and Coach Fischer were impressed with what had happened to the few and asked if Epley thought he could do the same for the whole team. Never lacking in self-confidence, Boyd volunteered that he thought he could, and thus was born Nebraska's strength-training program. Of course, Boyd, attempting to capitalize on the opportunity, pointed out that the facilities and the equipment were inadequate. He recommended that new purchases be made.

Who was this brash college junior who was so willing to step into an entirely new situation with such confidence of success? Boyd Epley came to Nebraska as a junior college transfer. He had been offered a track scholarship based on his pole-vaulting abilities. His weight-training knowledge and skills had developed earlier as an adjunct to his athletic activities.

Growing up in Arizona, Boyd had a friend, Pat Nevi, who introduced him to weights. Pat would lift weights any time he had the chance and this impressed Boyd. "He was more disciplined than anyone else I knew." Boyd, sixteen at the time, began to think that such a regimen might help him in football and track and so began lifting. Formal instruction in technique came from a neighbor, an elementary school teacher named Ken Cole, who was a lifter himself and ran a kind of lifters club in his garage. Boyd enjoyed his time with the lifters and the body builders but felt he had to develop his own program as an athlete, so he joined a health club. By the way, Boyd's young friend, Pat Nevi, went on to become Mr. America.

Epley admits that he didn't realize, at the time, that he was doing anything radical. He simply recognized that working with weights improved his performance on the field. His coaches weren't aware of what he was doing because his workouts were off campus and didn't interfere with his practices at school. Thus the knowledge he brought to Nebraska was mainly self-discovered and self-taught. Coming to NU, he never foresaw the role he would play in one of America's most successful football programs.

After getting the agreement of Coach Osborne and Fischer, the next step was getting the approval of Coach Devaney. With the backing of the two assistant coaches and of trainer George Sullivan, Epley's program carried the day. It began as an optional program for any player. When the 1969 season started, Epley was operating in a newly enlarged 1500-square-feet weight room. Over the summer, the old facility, one-third that size, had been expanded by knocking out a wall and including the area that had been a meeting room.

Epley remembers Mike "Red" Beran as being one of the first to respond to the optional program. Beran was a walk-on from Ord who lacked any impressive stats. When he began the program, Beran weighed 180 lbs. and ran the "40" in 5.5 seconds. His numbers were so unimpressive that Beran had been encouraged by the coaching staff to give up football. Working with Epley, Beran made unbelievable progress, raising his weight to 230 pounds while dropping his speed in the "40" to 4.9 seconds. At the same time, he increased his bench press from 220 pounds to 365. As Boyd modestly puts it, "That caught the eye of a lot of people." In 1984 Randy York, a *Lincoln Journal-Star* sportswriter, picked his "All Time Walk-On Team." Starting at offensive guard was Mike "Red" Beran.

Although Mike Beran was dedicated and worked hard for the results, in many ways Epley is correct when he states that Beran was "my first creation." Boyd developed the programs for Beran to follow and worked with him on all aspects of them. One of the impressive things about Epley is his willingness to learn. Recognizing that Beran had very poor flexibility, Boyd sought to improve it. Knowing little about how to achieve this goal, he went over to the Physical Education Department and questioned dance instructors who were noted for their flexibility. Both Beran and Epley wound up taking classes in Danish flexibility exercises.

Beran's success was impressive, but Boyd felt he had to gain more believers. To do this, he began to work with the name athletes on the team, the so-called stars. Johnny Rodgers became a real workhorse on the hip sled, and this helped Epley's credibility. Although he had gained some response from the success with Beran, Boyd recognized that "when a star made progress everyone noticed; when a walk-on made progress only a few noticed." This change in emphasis was important. "That was when the program really took off."

Another factor, developing at the same time, was also significant:

One other thing that really helped this program be accepted wasn't the job I was doing so much, but the fact we had an influx of junior college transfers— Bob Newton, Keith Wortman, Dick Rupert and Carl Johnson—from California and Arizona, where lifting was a little more common. They understood what I was trying to do and accepted it more than maybe the Nebraska boys did. They were way ahead of their time, really mature. That set the standard for the Nebraska boys.

That was the beginning. Since 1969 there have been many changes in the program. The major one, of course, was the switch from an optional to a mandatory training program in 1973. One of Tom Osborne's first decisions as head coach was to make this move. He had seen the results and now wanted to make the benefits more broadly based. The second major change was the upgrading of facilities to the point where Nebraska's Strength Complex is today second to none.

Boyd Epley has been around through this and has changed too. Inevitably, as more knowledge was gained, more changes occurred in the program. This learning process never stops. As Boyd puts it, "I learn all the time. We're just scratching the surface." Are there any limits to what can be done with the human body in the area of strength training? Not according to Epley. "We're just getting warmed up."

In terms of philosophy of training, Epley admits that a variety of opinions exists within the strength-training profession. Interestingly enough, he thinks

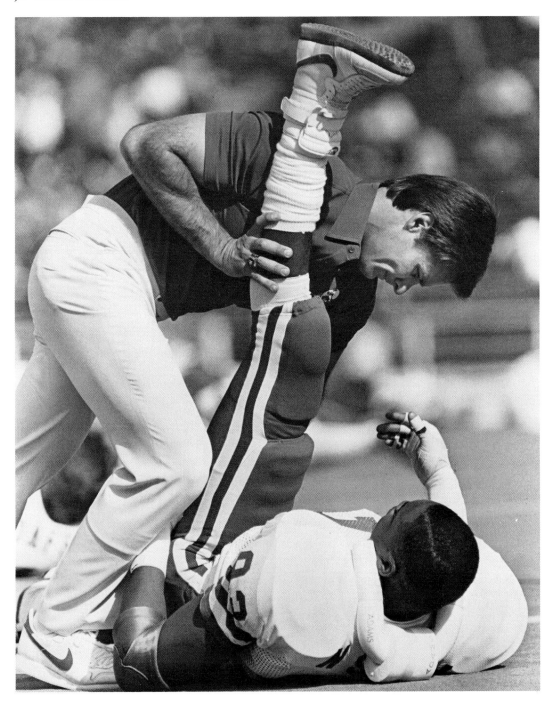

25. Boyd Epley helps
Neil Smith stretch out
before a game. Photo by
Dan Dulaney

the debate between supporters of "iron" and the supporters of machines has been overplayed. In his mind, iron, free weights, has it all over machines. "Most everyone involved in the strength training profession relies on iron. Machines do not produce strength at the same rate." The real differences in philosophy, Epley feels, are in how to use this iron.

Nebraska relies on the concept of "cycling." Epley believes that athletes do not have to train all-out every time they come to the weight room. During some periods of the year, less intensity is demanded, and during others athletes must train with greater intensity. Over the past couple of years, Epley and his staff have been doing a great deal of experimenting with this concept. One of the tools that has aided this pursuit of understanding has been the computer. It allows the staff to personalize each athlete's program and to monitor the results more closely. Fine tuning of the program is much easier with the aid of the computer than under previous methods of record-keeping and analysis.

Before a football player even enrolls at Nebraska, he is aware of the coaching staff's expectations in the area of conditioning. Epley meets with each recruit when he visits campus. Demonstrations are arranged and all sorts of literature distributed to familiarize the potential recruit with the Nebraska program. When he signs a letter of intent, a recruit receives a summer conditioning program to follow before his appearance on campus in the fall. For the overwhelming majority of recruits, weight or strength training is not something new. As early as junior high, players are introduced to weights by their coaches and many have been working out for several years before they reach college.

Epley points out, "Athletes are getting bigger and stronger naturally. They're getting better coaching earlier. They have better facilities and equipment." John Wen, in an article in the 1985 edition of *Athlon's Nebraska & Big Eight Football*, offered statistics to document this physical growth. In 1900 the average All-American lineman stood 6′1″ and weighed 195 pounds. By 1950 the average was 6′2½″ and 220 pounds, and in 1984, 6′4½″ and 268 pounds. Such statistics lead Epley to conclude: "The time is past when players can compete at our level at their natural sizes and strengths." As a result, performance is greatly enhanced. "Today's bench press for an average college team, not Nebraska, is over 300 pounds, as compared to 200–210 pounds fifteen years ago. The better teams average close to 350 pounds."

For every football player at the university, conditioning is a year-round proposition. When discussing this activity, Boyd likes to correct people who call it weight training. He prefers it described as strength training. The program includes more than simply working with iron; it includes speed drills and agility drills. "A much more serious approach than weight lifting." Consistent with the concept of "cycling," periods of greater and lesser activity alternate, but the goal is a better conditioned athlete at any time in the year.

During fall camp, players have a ten-day period when they don't work with weights. This coincides with the "two-a-days," and Epley feels that the players need time to recuperate and rebuild their bodies after the grueling sessions. During the season each player lifts approximately fifteen to twenty minutes a day after practice. A few, who have particularly heavy programs, may lift as long as thirty minutes. Another break occurs in December or January, when the players again have a month off. It follows the final game of the season and, as Epley notes, since the Huskers have played in a bowl game every season he has been strength coach, the rest is now taken for granted as occurring in January.

The players regroup at the end of January or the beginning of February to begin a six-week winter conditioning program. After listening to Epley describe the entire year's activities, one can only marvel at how tough this winter program is. Even Epley feels it is "an intense, demanding period." During this program, both conditioning and technique are emphasized. A normal week would be divided into two days of conditioning drills and two days of speed drills. In the speed drills, the stress is on technique. Simply put, this means teaching players how to run. Two areas are given heavy emphasis. First of all, players participate in power drills designed to increase stride length and then engage in drills designed to increase stride frequency. The conclusion is clear. If a player moves his legs faster and is covering more ground with each stride, he is, in effect, running faster.

After the winter conditioning program comes spring practice. The regular in-season schedule is maintained at this time. After spring ball, the players get another month off. Then comes a fifteen-week summer conditioning program. During these off-season sessions, players lift four days a week and run four days a week. The longest workout with weights would be an hour and a half, but that would be on top of a forty-minute running program.

The final bit of organization and philosophy comes with the establishment of control over the workouts themselves. Members of Boyd's staff are always on the floor, at the various weight stations, when the players are working out. They are there to monitor the workouts, to make sure the players are doing the exercises correctly, and also to sign the player's record to prove that he actually completed the prescribed routines. During the season each player follows a "four day split routine program." This means that it takes four days for each player to complete two entire repetitions of the program. In other words, the player works half the body each day, upper body one day, lower half the next. In the off season, the schedule calls for a "heavy-medium cycle." Here, early in the week, a heavy lifting schedule is maintained, and then later in the week a medium schedule is substituted. The entire cycle is completed in six weeks.

As with so many others on the football staff, Epley expresses amazement at how the program has grown over the last decade and a half. After beginning with a facility of 500 square feet, he now oversees the 13,300-square-feet "Strength Complex" that opened in 1979. This facility is so large that it can

26, 27. Thanks to solid coaching and strength training, when Danny Noonan sets his eyes on the quarterback, it's enough to knock his helmet off. Photos by Dan Dulaney

accommodate the entire football team, both varsity and freshman, at the same time with room to spare.

The increase in size has been accompanied by an increase in Epley's responsibilities. He has general oversight of the "Strength Complex" as well as the facilities in the Coliseum, on East Campus, and at the Bob Devaney Sports Center. Strength training for all intercollegiate teams fielded by the university comes under his jurisdiction. He also is responsible for all the weight training–body conditioning classes offered by the Physical Education Department. To fulfill these responsibilities, Epley is assisted by a staff of nine (the Physical Education Department furnishes the instructors for its classes). So specialized is some of the work that one of his assistants is in charge of "body composition." This means that he is responsible for players on special diets and for those attempting to lose weight and/or body fat. The assistant will go so far as to accompany the player through the cafeteria line to make sure the right foods get on his tray.

Epley shares something else with his university colleagues: money always seems in short supply. Projects and areas of improvement run far ahead of funding. One area of key concern is that of staff salaries. Over the past ten years Epley has lost sixteen assistants to head coaching positions. If he counts those who left not only for career advancement but also because of financial reasons, Boyd claims the number would be thirteen between 1983 and 1985. To help prevent such losses in the future and provide for new equipment purchases, Epley has organized the Husker Power Club to raise money outside of traditional university funds.

The people of Nebraska have responded to Boyd's needs. He estimates that he has spoken before every country club in the state and every university group, in his words, "from the dentists, to the doctors, to the farmers, to the engineers." He proudly points out to visitors the items that have come in to the "Strength Complex." With only slight exaggeration, he states, "Everything you see out there [in the complex] has been donated, including the computer."

With everything that he has accomplished, Epley sees more to do. He wants to purchase a new, more powerful computer, develop new software, raise staff salaries, obtain new equipment. To this end he is increasing his fund-raising activities. This will somehow be worked in on top of his already busy training schedule. Will he be able to do it? When presented with the question, he never even hesitates. With great pride in his voice, he declares that "Nebraska is the birthplace of strength training for athletes." Clearly, he will accept nothing but a leadership position for his institution. He is willing to work harder and learn more to keep NU on top. As he always tells his athletes, "The great ones adjust." You can believe him when he assures you: "The future looks bright for Nebraska."

Chapter Seven

Academic Counseling

Tom Osborne makes no bones about it, academics are an important part of the football experience at Nebraska. Such a position is not surprising when one considers that Tom Osborne holds both a master's degree and a doctor of philosophy degree from the University of Nebraska and, for a period, was an instructor in educational psychology at the university. When he became head coach, one of his first decisions was to hire Ursula Walsh as academic counselor for the football program. A lot has happened since that time, but Coach Osborne's reasoning, as expressed in *More Than Winning*, remains constant. "The first benefit of the academic counseling program is that it helps in recruiting. . . . Secondly, I think it's very important for the players to feel that they have someone who really cares about their academic progress and also is proficient in trying to discern their needs."

Dr. Walsh's name became synonymous with the academic counseling program, and even after she left in 1985 to accept an executive position with the National Collegiate Athletic Association, people continued to associate Ursula Walsh with the fine program she developed. As with all the people associated with the Nebraska program, the first thing that struck one about Ursula Walsh was her enthusiasm. Caring might be an overused word, but that was the attitude she conveyed.

She was quick to laugh when asked about the origins of her position. The story told by Coach Osborne about how Ursula criticized him for his handling of the study table is exaggerated, she claimed. After leaving a religious order, Dr. Walsh was in graduate school at Nebraska and attempting to find some way to augment her income. Living in Selleck dormitory, she saw how the study table was being run. Pursuing advanced degrees in education, she felt offended by the "chaotic" conditions and believed she could organize a better program.

Dr. Walsh readily admits that she had no burning interest in football or the team. She was simply looking for something to do. She contacted Tom Osborne, who at that time was the designated successor to Bob Devaney and the supervisor of the study table, and offered help in improving the program. Coach Osborne invited her over for a visit. In preparation for this meeting Dr. Walsh assembled flow charts and graphs along with other material to illustrate her points. Coach Osborne was so impressed, he offered her the position and the rest, as they say, is history.

When asked, Dr. Walsh found it somewhat difficult to define the position she created. As head academic counselor her responsibilities cut across simple job descriptions and academic lines. In her words, "We [had] a couple of purposes. We would like to see that everyone is happy and productive in the classroom. Anything that would impinge on the academics, I would consider my domain—problems with professors, personal problems, problems with coaches, anything at all."

Her contact with players began before they even made a commitment to come to Nebraska. The recruiting coordinator would notify her which potential recruits were coming in for a campus visit and what their academic interests were. Dr. Walsh and her assistants then put together informational packets that provided each visitor with facts about his potential major, course requirements, academic expectations of the coaching staff, and even possible courses the recruit would be taking in his freshman year. That meant that she discussed, individually, the academic futures of approximately ninety-five official recruits each year.

What was she hoping to find? Her goal was to determine their academic aspirations, to decide if we could "meet their needs." Dr. Walsh took this responsibility very seriously. If the university did not offer a major in which the recruit was interested, she would counsel him to go elsewhere. The famous story of Spencer Tillman, the Oklahoma running back, wanting to come to Nebraska but being discouraged by Dr. Walsh because NU had no major in petroleum engineering is, she assures one, very true.

At the beginning of the fall semester the work really began. When one counts the varsity players, redshirts, and freshman players, the number can be substantial. At the beginning of the 1985 season, for example, Dr. Walsh was working with 272 players. One point she stressed was that "we [didn't] really make distinctions between scholarship and non-scholarship players. They all get treated alike in [the counseling center]." Dr. Walsh would begin by reviewing the student's academic record and offering some diagnostic testing. Although Nebraska makes academic performance in high school an important criterion in determining whether or not to offer a scholarship, sometimes student-athletes do arrive on campus with academic deficiencies. In reflecting on the evaluation of recruits and the decision to offer a scholarship, Dr. Walsh felt: "If their skills are minimal but they're willing to work to make that up— that's OK. But we point[ed] that out to them. I never [said] no." One factor that some fans may not appreciate is the expense involved in upgrading some player's academic skills. For a program run on a budget like NU's, this is a factor. Dr. Walsh always "let the coaches know it [would] cost a lot of money to help a player out."

Like every student at UNL, each football player has a faculty member as an academic adviser. The player is encouraged to speak with his adviser and work out a schedule that will put him on the track toward graduation. Unlike the average student, however, football players have some special needs and requirements. For instance, the National Collegiate Athletic Association requires the completion of a form for each player associated with the program, giving evidence that he is meeting the organization's minimum academic requirements. Dr. Walsh was responsible for making sure these forms were completed and submitted on time. Meeting these requirements is not too difficult for Nebraska players because Coach Osborne has set standards above the NCAA minimum. Although the organization requires the completion of twenty-four credit hours toward a degree in an academic year, Nebraska players must complete thirty hours. Coach Osborne hopes to insure that graduation will be a reality for his players.

The academic counseling office runs mandatory study halls for players. Any player who has diagnostic test scores below a certain level or who has a grade point average below 2.3 (out of a possible 4.0) must attend. These study halls are held Monday through Friday mornings from 8:00 to 11:00 and Monday through Thursday evenings. Players must have at least six hours of supervised study but, as Dr. Walsh put it, "more made us happy." At the evening study halls, tutors in all the major subjects are present to assist the players.

Another problem unique to student athletes is the necessity of scheduling classes that don't conflict with team meetings and practices. With the wide-ranging offerings of a major university, this problem can usually be avoided, but on occasion it has necessitated a player being excused from practice to attend a lab or a class that he needs to fulfill the requirements of his major. Coach Osborne has always been understanding in this regard. At times, this type of conflict has been circumvented by clearing it with a professor to hire his graduate assistant to conduct a special lab for the player(s) involved.

In talking with Dr. Walsh, one senses the great satisfaction she draws from her accomplishments. Looking back over her thirteen years in the program she found it hard to believe all that had happened. The academic counseling office, like the whole football program, has grown larger and more complex. With a wistful look in her eye, she said, "It was so small when I started [1972]. [By 1985] there are people in the program I don't even know."

When asked how she would define success in terms of her job, Dr. Walsh again found it difficult to be specific. At first she said, "I want[ed] them [the players] to be perfect." Then she laughed and admitted that this isn't a practical goal. The easiest measure of success to quantify would be the number of players graduated. Over the years, Nebraska has had one of the highest graduation rates among major college football programs. Dr. Walsh noted that in this regard, "Redshirting [was] a blessing for me." It gave the players an extra year to complete academic requirements. This is one way of determining success. But Dr. Walsh wasn't happy with it. For some players, being associated with a program like Nebraska's and spending five years on campus in Lincoln is a tremendous shaping experience, even if they don't graduate. For those people, graduation can't be the sole measure of success. After a time she admitted that maybe there just wasn't a simple way of determining success.

Just as there are All-Star teams for players who have demonstrated prowess on the playing field, there is an All-Star team for student athletes who have excelled in both sports and academics. If one counts how many All-Americans the Nebraska coaches have produced, one should also recognize that Nebraska players have had more than their share of academic recognition too. Since 1960 the Cornhuskers have had twenty-nine football players designated as Academic All-Americans by the College Sports Information Directors of America. Nineteen of those recognized benefited from the programs set up by Dr. Walsh. Lest some think that these players were not among the "superstars," the list includes such names as Dennis Claridge, Tony Jeter, Jeff Kinney, Larry Jacobson, Rik Bonness, Vince Ferragamo, George Andrews, Kelly Saalfeld, Dave Rimington, and Mark Traynowicz.

After Dr. Walsh accepted the position with the National Collegiate Athletic Association, the Athletic Department used this opportunity to redefine the responsibilities of the academic counselor. Al Papik now directs the program and performs additional duties as special assistant to the athletic director. Marsha Shada has taken over most of Dr. Walsh's day-to-day dealings with the football players.

Dr. Walsh expressed real regret in leaving Nebraska but felt "it was time to move on. To get on with my life." Ursula had nothing but praise for the athletic program in Lincoln. In her words, the program is "absolutely first class from top to bottom." The time she spent at Nebraska was rewarding because "it's wonderful to be associated with excellence." When asked how she would sum up her experience, what advice would she try to impress upon student athletes, she responded that she had always offered the same definition of a happy life: "Using your talents in a life that gives them scope."

Chapter Eight

The Cornhuskers on the Road

Of the many memories of the players interviewed, one common experience overshadows all the others. Whether one speaks with a player from the 1920s or the 1980s, each is likely to mention the travel involved with the football program. From the leisurely pace of cross-country train trips to the speed of jet planes, the road trips are well remembered. The bonding ritual of teamwork is intensified by the isolation and proximity induced by travel. For many boys from small towns and modest circumstances, travel opened windows on the world never to be forgotten.

From the earliest days of the program, Nebraska squads traveled to find the best competition. For many, the trips were almost like fairy tales, but for others reality intruded. An incident involving George Flippin, Nebraska's black half-back from the early 1890s, illustrates both the unpleasantness that could occur and the support he received from his college classmates. The incident involved the road trip to Denver described in Chapter 1. The student newspaper, the *Hesperian*, took a different view of the hospitality that the *Nebraska State Journal* had found so worthy of comment:

Imagine our surprise when we received word from Denver that our colored player had been refused admittance to the parquet portion of the Opera House in Denver. Through a false idea of patronage, the manager of the opera house got the idea into his bigoted brain, devoid of gray matter, that his patrons would not like to see a negro in the fashionable part of the opera house. That a city as far west as Denver should contain men with such poor judgment and prejudicial feeling is certainly astonishing. The remainder of our club, of course, then refused to attend the play. In this they did right. Mr. Flippin is a member of our team and a student of our University. This latter fact entitles him to all the rights and privileges enjoyed by any other student. Whatever he is not allowed to do the other members of the team will not do. So anyone as narrow-minded as the manager of the Denver Opera House may as well come off his perch and associate with white people, even though their color may be black.

Over the years, the happy memories far overshadow the unpleasant ones. Travel was broadening and exciting, particularly during the age of the railroad. Everyone who experienced them remembers the train trips to the away games. Especially for the players of the pre–World War II era, these are memories still cherished. Bob Benson probably summed it up for all the former Cornhuskers when he said: "The train trips were part of my growing up." Even Lloyd Cardwell, the toughest of the tough, when asked about his fondest memory of his days as a Husker, recalled the 1936 trip to Oregon State and having "a special train of our own."

The comments have a consistency that helps to explain the memories. Glen Presnell remembers, "The wonderful trips were great for a boy who had never been east of Omaha or west of Kearney." Ladas Hubka, who played from 1933 to 1935, feels, "The trips which we took by rail were very pleasant in the experience of a country hay shaker who had never been very far from home [Table Rock, Nebraska]." Jack Ashburn, a member of the Cornhusker squads from 1937 to 1939, echoes the same sentiment. "I came from a small town [Tilden, Nebraska] and had never been away from home very far and the football trips to Pittsburgh, Minnesota, Iowa, Indiana on the trains were very memorable. It gave us a chance to see professional football games and baseball games in Chicago and the practices in Soldiers Field in Chicago."

It doesn't take long for the players, when pressed further about their memories of these trips, to get around to the food served in the dining cars and hotels. Young men trying to work their way through college during the Depression and play football too didn't always have a lot of time or money to spend on food. When asked if he would change anything about his days as a Husker, Bob Mehring commented, "If they had only had a training table or given us food money, it would have helped so much." Player after player remembers living on beans and potatoes, or chili, or eggs from the family farm. Football, 1930s style, didn't include the scientific evaluation of nutritional needs that the players experience today. This may be why Forrest Behm, an All-American tackle in 1940, recalled the best memories as "returning to Lincoln on a train after we won. I loved those train rides and having breakfast in a diner. That was really living."

For each trip the players received a detailed itinerary, and menus especially printed for the occasion accompanied each meal aboard the train. The longest trips were those to either coast. For the players on the 1936 squad, the trip to play Oregon State is one that was never topped.

A check of the menus from this trip bears out the players' contention that the food was something out of the ordinary. On both Thursday, the 26th, and Friday, the 27th, the breakfast menu aboard the Union Pacific car offered a choice of orange juice, stewed prunes, baked apple with cream, tomato juice, half a grapefruit, or kadota figs with cream. Then another choice followed.

Players selected among oatmeal, cream of wheat, Grape-Nuts, All-Bran, shredded wheat biscuit, or corn flakes with cream. Then came two eggs any style, broiled sugar-cured ham or bacon, or calf's liver sautéed. Included was a selection of hot rolls, corn muffins, and toast with apple butter. To wash down all the food, the players had a choice of coffee, tea, milk, cocoa, or noncaffeine coffee.

The luncheon menus offer more of the same. The one for Thursday, the 26th, was typical. The meal began with Beef Broth Anglaise, followed by a choice of barbecued black cod with drawn butter, braised tenderloin of beef Jardinere, or baked sugar-cured ham with raisin sauce. Served with the entree were potatoes Persillade and brussels sprouts. A fruit salad complemented the main course. For dessert the players could choose pineapple sherbet with wafers or a baked apple with cream. Accompanying this was a choice of coffee, tea, milk, or cocoa. The pattern of dishes was maintained throughout the trip but with great variety. Another day the soup was tomato bouillon and the choice of entrees included fillet of halibut tartare, grilled lamb chops, or roast prime rib of beef au jus.

Dinners consisted of more of the same fine food. For this meal, the players usually partook of a common menu. Aboard a Burlington train on the return from the game, the December 1 dinner consisted of a relish tray of Colorado pascal celery and select olives, followed by a Puree-Mongole. The main course was a broiled dinner steak accompanied by a baked potato and string beans with a lettuce-tomato salad with Sauce-Dumont and hot dinner rolls. For dessert was apple pie a la mode and cheese with crackers. From this typical fare, one can see why the players were so anxious to travel to away games and why the memory of the meals remains after almost half a century.

28. A half century later, Forrest Behm still remembers the train trips. Courtesy of the Nebraska State Historical Society

29. A menu from those memorable train trips. Photo by Dan Dulaney

FORREST BEHM, Tackle

Forrest will wind up with another great year as a Cornhusker. Big and aggressive, weighs 200 lbs., stands 6-4. Lincoln is his home.

Luncheon

TOMATO BOUILLON

CELERY   CARROT STICKS

FILET OF HALIBUT, TARTARE
GRILLED LAMB CHOPS
ROAST PRIME RIBS OF BEEF, AU JUS

STEAMED POTATOES   GREEN BEANS

PINEAPPLE AND COTTAGE CHEESE SALAD

VANILLA ICE CREAM, SWEET WAFERS

COFFEE   TEA   MILK   COCOA

University of Nebraska
Football Team
and Party

Under the direction of
Coach Dana X. Bible

En Route
Portland, Oregon

November 25, 1936

Even the day trips could be exciting and the food above the ordinary. In 1937 the Cornhuskers played a Big Six game at Kansas State. Considering how conscious coaches are today of overloading players with heavy food, it is interesting to note that the itinerary called for three meals on the trip:

ITINERARY

to Manhattan, Kans.—November 27, 1937

Saturday, November 27th

7:30 A.M.	Leave Lincoln on Union Pacific Railroad
7:35 A.M.	Breakfast, private diner
11:45 A.M.	Lunch, private diner
11:45 A.M.	Arrive at Manhattan
12:15 P.M.	Taxi to Stadium
2:00 P.M.	Game
4:30 P.M.	Taxi to Train
5:30 P.M.	Dinner, private diner
7:10 P.M.	Leave Manhattan
11:25 P.M.	Arrive Lincoln

Those were full-sized meals too, not just tea and toast. Breakfast consisted of juice, dry cereal, and eggs with a choice of ham, bacon, or a small breakfast steak. Four hours later, approximately two hours before kickoff, the players sat down to a lunch of roast prime rib of beef with poached eggs and a baked potato, all washed down with tea and orange juice. For dinner, probably less than two hours after the game ended, the menu called for cream of tomato soup, roast Nebraska turkey with baked potato and vegetables, Waldorf salad, and dessert. When you had the chance to eat like this only a few times a year, you didn't pass it up.

The food in the hotels was of comparable quality and quantity. When reminiscing about these trips, Bob Benson got a faraway look in his eyes and commented, "I had my first baked potato at the William Penn Hotel in Pittsburgh. It was so big it must have weighed a pound." Player after player commented on the William Penn in Pittsburgh or the Palmer House in Chicago. These hotels were places guaranteed to widen the eyes of the boys from Nebraska.

Food isn't the only memory the players have of these trips. Since the players were away from campus for several days at a time, the administration attempted to make the trips as educational as possible. The itinerary for the Oregon State game and for a trip the following season to Pittsburgh includes several stops for sight-seeing and learning. Players visited Indian reservations, natural wonders, professional ball games, and theaters.

Not all the stops were preplanned. Several players mentioned how stops would be made if something of interest was passed. Indian reservations, national parks, historic monuments were all possible stopping sights. Such flexibility was possible because the Cornhuskers usually traveled in their own cars and sometimes even their own trains. More than one player from the 1930s mentioned that the president of the Burlington and the president of the Union Pacific were both Nebraska fans and would attach their private cars to the Cornhusker trains to travel to the games. With such clout as this around, no wonder the players got special treatment.

The 1936 Oregon State trip is a classic example. On the way back to Lincoln, while still in the mountains of Montana, William Jeffers, the president of the Union Pacific, had the train stopped. All the players were given the opportunity to chop down Christmas trees for their families. Several players remember managing to fill a boxcar with freshly cut trees. On this same trip, the train stopped in Grand Island so that Bob Mehring, Les McDonald, and some others could get off in their hometown. Mehring describes standing on the platform, jokingly calling up to Bill Jeffers. "Mr. Jeffers, I think I got cheated." When the railroad president asked how, Mehring responded, "I was supposed to travel round trip to Lincoln and here I am getting off in Grand Island." Jeffers told him to wait a minute and ducked back inside his car. Coming back on the platform, he flipped something to Mehring saying that that should make them even. It was a book of passes for the Union Pacific Railroad. Mehring appreciated the gesture but recalled that he never used them. After all, hitchhiking to Lincoln was faster than taking the train. "All you had to do was wear your N sweater and the first car along gave you a ride."

Fans sometimes traveled on the same trains as the players. Since the popularity of Cornhusker football was intense, very often faithful followers would want to go to the away games. Again, the trip to Oregon State serves as a case in point. The Union Pacific and Burlington put together a special train and advertised it in a liberally illustrated brochure featuring a picture of Lloyd Cardwell on the front. Inside was information on sightseeing and the game and descriptions of the routes. The train was the one the Huskers were traveling on and thus would leave on Wednesday, November 25, and return Wednesday, December 2. Round-trip group fares for the excursion were $41.80 per person in tourist Pullman sleeping cars and $62.69 per person in standard Pullman sleeping cars.

A menu from the Great Northern Railway illustrates the cost of food for these fans. The "Chef's Suggestion Plate Number Three," for instance, cost $.50. It included meat or fish, potatoes and one other vegetable, "all served on a large plate, family style," bread and butter, and coffee, tea, or milk. The menu informed the diner: "Steward or waiter will gladly, on request, advise as to kind of meat 'Chef' is featuring today." As a final note the menu promised "a second portion of any item, served on request, no additional charge." If a traveler wanted to order off the A *La Carte* side, a lamb or pork chop cost $.30 while a sirloin steak was $1.00.

A final interesting point, from the perspective of the 1980s, is that not a single player mentioned boredom as a factor on these trips. Scenery was plentiful and one could always look forward to the stops. A well-established ritual was always followed aboard the trains. First-year players were expected to carry the luggage, sleep in the upper bunks, and entertain the upper classmen. Many players mentioned this aspect with fondness, likening it to a fraternity.

The overriding recollection described by these former Cornhuskers was that of camaraderie. Time and time again, someone would mention how close he was to his teammates. It wasn't a case of a special friendship with one or two others, but rather an intense bonding among all the players. Of course, traveling squads in the 1930s averaged about thirty-five players and this small size aided the bonding process. In talking with these men half a century later, one can't help but sense the enthusiasm and true pleasure each received from his experiences on these trips.

Not just the players of the 1920s and 1930s have fond memories of the travel experience. Richard Moore believes his fondest memory as a Husker is "travelling to Miami Beach after the '54 season to play the Orange Bowl game. Just a great personal experience for a Corn Belt farm boy." Although Moore played two decades after Ladas Hubka, travel had the same effect on him.

Bill Kosch, a decade and a half after Richard Moore, carries the theme of the experience of travel into the national championship years. When asked about his most pleasant memories as a player, he responded, "I always enjoyed road trips and the day before the game. Practice took place during late afternoon on a new stage. We always had a steak, baked potato, green beans and ice cream for the pre-game meal. ALWAYS! Took in a movie, short chalk-talk and hit the rack."

Of course, someone has to take responsibility for making the arrangements and coordinating all the travel plans. At Nebraska, this someone is Gary Fouraker, the Athletic Department business manager. He makes the hotel reservations, charters the buses and planes, and consults with Tom Osborne and the trainers about what kind of equipment will be needed in the rooms and what type of meals will be served and the scheduling of those meals. The last thing the coaches need is to assemble their players and find out that the room lacks a chalkboard or a projector, or for the trainers to prepare to tape ankles before practice only to notice that there are no tables for the athletes to sit on for the procedure.

The business manager must also concern himself with some intangibles. Requesting so many chalkboards or rooms with running water to hook up the whirlpools is easy enough, but he also must consider the type of team Nebraska is fielding that year. Again, after discussions with Coach Osborne, Fouraker's arrangements may be influenced by the number of returning lettermen on the squad. "If it's a young team, you like to get them there early and enable them to familiarize themselves with the area. If the players have been there before, you don't need to bring them in so early." He also has to remember if the team had any problems at a hotel so that they won't be repeated. Those problems could range from poor service, to disregard for instructions, to noise. As one might expect, Fouraker mentioned Norman, Oklahoma, as an area where the Cornhuskers sometimes want to stay farther away from the field than usual to ensure a quiet evening before the game.

Preparations for away games, not including bowl games, can also illustrate the changes in the way the trainer operates. Some things remain constant. Each player packs his own bag. Into the bag go helmet, mouthpiece, and shoes. Since players have many different styles of shoes for natural and artificial turf, the trainer has to inform them of the type of playing surface so that the proper shoes will be packed. Beyond that, the trainer is responsible for everything else. One point that George Sullivan made was how the medical services have improved since he began his career. Almost every stadium in which the Huskers play has a portable x-ray machine that allows for a speedier evaluation and more rapid treatment of injuries. Also, the physical facilities themselves are better. Each team provides the visiting squad with tables, whirlpools, and other modern-day requirements. Aside from uniforms, Sullivan brings two large trunks of pads, sponges, tape, and assorted other protective gear to an away game.

Every fan knows about the "home field advantage," and every coach will tell you that he would rather play at home. However, for the players, travel adds an important element to the experience of participating in major college football. After the cheers have stopped and the body can't perform the magic it once could, the memories of those days on the road remain.

Chapter Nine

The Business of Football

College football involves the fans, the coaches, and the players. To be the spectacle, the event, that it is for so many, all these ingredients must be present. However, there are other factors necessary for the whole program to work the way it should. In particular, one must consider the financial side of the game and the publicity or public relations aspects.

The Athletic Department's business manager is responsible for making all the arrangements for team travel, balancing the books, attempting to keep all programs within budget, and simple fiscal oversight of the entire Athletic Department operation. At Nebraska, the man who holds this title is Gary Fouraker. After serving the University of Nebraska in a variety of staff positions for over a decade, Fouraker assumed his present position in 1981.

If the matter is related to finances and it comes into or goes out of the Athletic Department, Gary is responsible for it. In consultation with Athletic Director Bob Devaney and the individual team coaches, he helps to prepare the budget. He and his staff then monitor the application of those budget funds to insure compliance with university regulations and proper business procedures. Considering that for academic year 1985–86 the Athletic Department budget totaled $10,351,700, this is quite a responsibility.

A second hat worn by Fouraker is that of concessions director. He is responsible for all the vendors at Memorial Stadium on game days as well as vendors at all athletic contests throughout the year. On a normal football Saturday, approximately nine hundred people work concessions in Memorial Stadium. Included in this number are the preparers and sellers of food, as well as the program and souvenir vendors. When asked how one can prepare the proper amount of food for a football crowd, Fouraker grinned, shrugged, and said, "Experience and luck."

Weather can have a significant impact on sales. Warmer weather means more pop sales and less food sales. Cold weather brings just the opposite demand. Fouraker gets weather reports all week to try to estimate the amounts of food needed. Another factor influencing sales is the time of the game. "In recent years with the shifting of game times, we've had some problems. Anytime kickoff isn't at 1:30 we find our sales declining. The later the start, the more likely people are to eat at home or downtown on their way to the game." Those fluctuations can be significant and costly. When one considers that on the average home-game Saturday sixteen thousand hot dogs, six thousand Runzas and one thousand hamburgers are sold, the revenues generated are substantial. Over the course of a year, concessions account for $550,000 in income for the Athletic Department.

A good deal of flexibility and fluctuation is characteristic of the football budget, which in 1985–86 amounted to $5,000,000. Figuring out the cost of a traveling squad of sixty making a road trip to Columbia, Missouri, presents few problems, but how about budgeting for recruiting costs? During the time of the year when budget is developed, Coach Osborne has little idea where the best prospects will be. If Nebraska and Iowa have a bumper crop of blue chip players, recruiting costs will be low. What happens, however, if the best players that season are from New Jersey and California? Bringing ninety-five potential recruits in for their official visits can prove very costly if the majority are being flown in from the two coasts. Fouraker's job is to keep the coaching staff aware of expenditures and revenues remaining. As he so succinctly put it, "Our funds aren't unlimited. If the staff overspends in one area, they have to make it up in another."

Looking at the future, Gary Fouraker is concerned about a couple of matters. One is very predictable and the other may surprise some people. The first is the increasing amount of paper work required of his office. The National Collegiate Athletic Association, the university's Board of Regents, the federal government, and the state government are all demanding the production of new and increasingly detailed reports. Given the staff and the time required to comply with these demands, the resources of the office are being stretched thin.

The second problem is financial. Although a relatively new one, Fouraker can't claim that it is unique to the Athletic Department. Recent budget problems on the state level have caused the university's athletic programs to depend more heavily on private contributions for funding programs and purchasing equipment. Although Nebraska fans are well noted for the support they give their Huskers, Fouraker offers a surprising fact: "Donations to the athletic program at Nebraska are not comparable to those of other schools in the conference." Reasons for this have little or nothing to do with spirit but rather center around certain realities about the area itself. Nebraska doesn't have the population base that some other Big Eight states do. The Nebraska economy is closely aligned to the status of the farming community and recent downturns in the agricultural sector have made it increasingly difficult for people to give.

While conceding that the times make fund-raising more difficult, the man responsible for the actual solicitation of donations for the Athletic Department

30, 31. Whether the
wind chill is below zero
or the temperature and
humidity are over 100,
the Husker faithful cheer
on the Scarlet and
Cream. Photos by Dan
Dulaney

is more upbeat than the business manager in his assessment. Lee Liggett, a retired brigadier general, is vice president of the University of Nebraska Foundation. For the better part of the last decade, he has traveled in state and out of state seeking donors for the university's athletic programs. If any man has a bird's-eye view of the situation, it is Liggett.

Lee Liggett, a native of Utica, Nebraska, finds that his fellow Nebraskans want to donate to the football program. "There's something about Nebraskans; they really love their football." Building on this sense of pride and interest, supporters are organized in various clubs and groups. Liggett was quick to point out that because of Nebraska's success and consequent record of consecutive home-game sellouts, fund-raisers are unable to offer tickets as an inducement for donations. He would love to have that as a bargaining tool, but tickets are simply not available. Helen Ruth Wagner, the ticket manager, was quick to support this. No one is ever promised tickets in return for a contribution.

Liggett feels the reasons for giving center around intangibles. As he put it, "Nebraska isn't blessed with beautiful mountains or large lakes. Football, and the university in general, give Nebraskans a sense of pride. It really gives you a lift to walk into a meeting in New York or Dallas or Chicago and have somebody say 'How's the football team this year?'." Nebraskans have a loyalty to their sports teams. This can be seen with the local high school squads and, Liggett feels, it carries right over to the Cornhuskers.

Whether giving is more or less difficult for Nebraska supporters is a question of dispute, but certainly there are two points on which Fouraker and Liggett agree. First of all, Nebraskans are willing to give and there is no substitute for enthusiasm. Secondly, contributions play a significant role in the athletic programs of the University of Nebraska. Gary Fouraker stated unequivocally that "donations are important for maintaining quality programs." He anticipated that approximately $800,000 would be raised from contributions in 1985–86.

To increase and sustain private contributions to the Nebraska Athletic Department in general, and the football program in particular, a number of organizations dedicated to fund-raising have assumed an increased importance. The most expensive to which to belong is the Director's Club. To qualify for membership here, one must contribute a minimum of $50,000 to the program over a ten-year period or arrange for a deferred gift of $100,000 or more. Founded in 1981 and open to both individual and corporate members, the Director's Club has been successful in developing several substantial donors for the program. Of course, as Lee Liggett points out, although the Director's Club has been "very successful, it has a limited clientele."

Less expensive is the Husker Award Club. The club, founded in 1960, originally required an annual contribution of $1,000 for membership. Recognizing a growing need and reality, the club changed the terms of membership in

1983. Now three levels of membership exist within the club. The gold level requires a $2,000 annual contribution, the silver a $1,000, and the bronze a $500 annual contribution. Finally, there is the Touchdown Club. The Touchdown Club developed among some fans in the late 1950s and came under university control and direction in 1964. Originally, annual membership dues were $100 a year. In 1979 they were raised to $150 and in 1982 to $200 a year.

Some special-interest clubs are also associated with the program. The Wheel Club's membership consists of new-car dealers who donate the use of cars for the football staff. Formed in 1962, the Beef Club originally involved ranchers and feedlot operators willing to contribute a minimum of $100 a year to the program. The club based this contribution on the older practice of donating beef for the training table. The Athletic Department reasoned that contributions in cash can be more easily managed than contributions in kind. Today the club is geared to those Cornhusker supporters who live outstate or have ties to the agricultural community. Very rarely does someone now offer the Business Office a steer for its use. Instead, membership in the Beef Club can be acquired for a minimum contribution of $200 annually.

Although sometimes broader in purpose than simple support of the football program, the various state clubs also play a role. Look around the stadium on any given Saturday and you will see banners proclaiming "Georgians for Nebraska," "Alaskans for Nebraska," "North Texans for Nebraska," and many others, including the most famous, "Californians for Nebraska." In 1963 the "Californians for Nebraska" club chartered its first flight to a home game. The group helps to raise money for various athletic endeavors in addition to its sponsorship of trips and rallies. It also helps to maintain the Nebraska presence in a state that has furnished the Huskers with many outstanding players.

Although Gary Fouraker wears many hats, he has only one goal in mind. That is achieving and maintaining the financial solidity of the Nebraska Athletic Program. Although not easy, and at times frustrating, it is something that has to be done if the Cornhuskers are to maintain their preeminent position in the world of college athletics.

At least Gary Fouraker is dealing with concrete facts and figures. If it takes so many dollars to pay for a project then the budget needs to reflect this. Don Bryant in the Sports Information Department at the university has a more difficult problem to address. Put as simply as possible, Bryant and his staff have the responsibility of letting the world know what is happening in Nebraska athletics. Given the number of colleges and universities competing in intercollegiate athletics, the amount of "press" any one will receive is limited. Bryant wants to make sure Nebraska gets everything it deserves.

Bryant is only the second full-time sports information director at the University of Nebraska. Greg McBride, a sportswriter for both Lincoln and Omaha newspapers, handled the chores on a part-time basis, and then after World War

32–37. Fans travel from near and far to salute their Cornhuskers. Photos by Dan Dulaney

II John Bently took over full-time responsibility. When Bryant left his job as sports editor of the *Lincoln Star* in 1963 to become sports information director, some of his friends kidded him about going into retirement. Today no one would belittle or underestimate the job he has done, or has yet to do. As the success and national recognition of Cornhusker athletic programs have grown, so have the duties of the position. At present, in addition to Bryant, the staff consists of three full-time assistants, two secretaries, and three student assistants. The office handles the publicity of eighteen men's and women's university teams.

As an example of the growth of responsibility and interest, one has only to refer to the Nebraska press guide. Originally developed to help working journalists cover Cornhusker football teams, the media guide is now a hot item with the Husker fans. Around eight thousand copies a year are sold to the general public. The office also maintains a mailing list of over six hundred names of individuals and media outlets, which receive press releases generated by Bryant's staff. Every press release goes out to at least one media representative in every state in the United States.

The Sports Information Office sets up interviews with players and coaches, secures housing for visiting media, and makes decisions on awarding media passes for Husker events. A football game of national significance can attract requests for media credentials numbering near one thousand. Although the press box at Memorial Stadium has some of the best facilities available anywhere, the number of spaces is still limited. For the 1984 Nebraska-Oklahoma game, the Sports Information Office issued six hundred sets of media credentials.

Bob Devaney appreciates the effort and the return. He is quick to point out that the Sports Information Department has made a significant contribution to Nebraska's parade of All-Americans, particularly offensive linemen. As the athletic director notes, "The people who vote for the [All-America] teams can watch film of running backs and receivers and make their selections, but evaluating linemen is much more difficult. The Sports Information Office can bring these people to the attention of the voters. Skill still should be the determining factor, but they [the voters] need to know who to look at."

Tom Simons, the associate sports information director, is pleased that Coach Devaney sees the department as making such a contribution, but quickly points out that there is "no real system" employed by the Sports Information Department in this regard. Tom categorically states, "We've never really launched an all out campaign to win an award for anybody."

When asked to explain Nebraska's record for turning out All-American linemen, Simons feels it all goes back to the overall success of the program. "Voters are smart enough to recognize the contributions of the linemen. They know that Johnny Rodgers or Mike Rozier needed people in front of them opening up holes." When a team is gaining better than four hundred yards a game in total offense, voters focus in on it. Over the years success breeds success. Schools gain a reputation for turning out excellent players in certain positions. When voters are seeking individuals to consider for All-American linemen, they naturally look to Nebraska.

Although Nebraska doesn't launch poster campaigns or special press release mailings, the SID's staff is "always on the lookout for good quotes about the offensive linemen." Tom notes, "Our coaches have always spoken very positively about our linemen." Opposing coaches' remarks and media com-

38. Preparation for the half-time show is not without its dangers, as the cheerleader's wrapped thigh indicates. Photo by Dan Dulaney

39. But the appreciation of 76,000 fans makes all the effort worth it. Photo by Dan Dulaney

ments are also closely monitored for mention of the linemen. These quotes are then assembled in the pregame notes distributed to the press attending the game. Televised games help boost the credentials of potential award winners. The SID's staff makes sure the TV people know who the top linemen are so that they can focus on them. In a nationally televised game, isolated replays of the interior line play can go far in boosting the credentials of outstanding linemen. As Tom Simons notes, "Our players have never let us down yet." When all is said and done, Tom believes the worthy players still get the awards. "No one has ever won the Heisman, Lombardi or Outland Trophy because his Sports Information Department put out a better poster or wrote more letters."

The hours are long and the demands can be great, but you don't hear Don Bryant complaining. He realizes that the increased work is the result of the success of Nebraska athletic programs. He would much rather have Nebraska winning and his office swamped than have all the time in the world and a losing football team.

40. Bob Mehring in 1986. Only members of league champions were allowed to wear the white letter sweater. Note the championship ring on his left hand. Photo by Dan Dulaney

Chapter Ten

An Experience That Molds Your Life

Throughout the story of the Huskers one can't help but notice how much of the experience players remember. Although all the memories may not be pleasant, the sheer quantity of them is impressive. Looking back, one has to wonder if the experience was worth it. Did the players bring anything into their adult lives from their days as players? If they had it to do over again, would they still play football? When this question was presented to former players, many responded in great depth and detail. A decade, or two, or five has not clouded the memories or dimmed the impressions. All the experiences did not take place on the playing field. For many, the ones with greatest impact took place outside the arena or after the playing days were through.

For some, the greatest memory is the one of actually making the team, the rush of emotion that accompanied the realization of a long cherished hope. Bob Mehring's account of his first practices in 1935 may be the most emotional of the responses, but the expression of exhilaration is general and is consistent through the decades. Dave Butterfield, who played from 1972 to 1976, offers an example of this enthusiasm. Playing for Nebraska "was a fantastic experience, a dream come true. I wanted to play for Nebraska from the first time I saw them play in 1964 against Kansas."

Other memories include jokes that teammates played on one another, or the special times they shared in preparing for games or in recovering from losses. Al Zikmund still gets shivers up his spine, forty years later, remembering the preparations before home football contests. The players spent the night before the game at the National Guard camp in Ashland:

They'd feed us a real good meal and then show us a movie. It'd always be a comedy that we'd split our sides laughing at. In the morning we'd have a real big breakfast—cream of wheat or oatmeal and a small steak. Just before we left for the stadium we'd have a pre-game meal—tea, toast with honey, and oranges with powdered sugar. After we got on the bus, Link [Lyman] would start singing 'Come a Running Boys' and the emotions would get so high most of the team would lose their tea and toast.

Individual players recall particular moments in their careers that have stayed with them. Bill Kosch describes one of the more moving memories.

Johnny Rodgers always produced. To me, personally, his greatest deed was off the field. After the 1971 Orange Bowl, JR was awarded the game ball. He deserved it in all respects. One of our team members, Rex Lowe, was confined to a wheel chair, physically deteriorating, and was with us in the locker room. This is when JR made his greatest move with a football. As he started to talk, a rare moment of silence occurred as he approached Rex. He said Rex had fought harder than any of us to make it to this point in life. He presented Rex the game ball. There were genuine tears shed by many of us. I never told Johnny, but his actions, him being 'JR Superstar' earned a lot of respect. The action could have been ignored. But that event will be memorialized in my mind forever.

Tom "Train Wreck" Novak offers an example of the kind of personal memories that are so private and sometimes so special that others would never realize they existed unless told. When asked what his most special memory of his days as a Husker was, Tom Novak responded: "The 1949 halftime program honoring my birthday. Everyone sang 'Happy Birthday'." Not the sort of memory one would associate with one of the meanest, toughest Huskers ever to wear the Scarlet and Cream.

No questioning of former players about their memories would be complete without some reference to great players and great games. Some of the players felt they couldn't choose among opponents or teammates because so many were deserving of praise. Others were more willing to put their neck on the line and offer an opinion. Some of the answers are surprising and some would surprise no one.

Each of the players interviewed was asked his opinion of the greatest game in Husker history. They were not limited to games in which they had participated and could, if they so desired, offer a justification for their choice. The majority opinion offers no surprise. The 1971 Nebraska-Oklahoma "Game of the Century" was far and away the choice of the majority. Adrian Fiala probably articulated the sentiment best:

Both teams were nationally ranked. Both teams were statistical leaders in the nation; multiple talents on each team. Played on a classic Fall afternoon with everything on the line and subject to the most pre-game hype that radio, TV and press could give. The game . . . , in my opinion, exceeded all expectations. This is unique in that usually the games which get all the pregame hype fall far below expectations and sometimes just fail miserably. . . . The game had absolutely every element which I feel represents the epitome of college football.

Although the overwhelming choice, the "Game of the Century" was not the only one offered. Some of the players remember the titanic struggles with Notre

Dame in the 1920s. Both the 1922 and 1923 games had their supporters. Nebraska-Minnesota contests also had their fans, particularly the 1937 Nebraska victory. Two former players cast their votes for the 1936 Nebraska-Indiana game, in which Nebraska was down 0–9 before coming back in the fourth quarter to record a 13–9 victory. The Rose Bowl game had its champions, as did the two Orange Bowls where Nebraska gained its national championships. Finally, some players chose games that were special to them and thus, they felt, special to the program. An example would be Dave Shamblin's choice of the 1978 Oklahoma-Nebraska game. Dave's reason: "We won by wanting to win more than they did. They had much more talent, we had much more will to win."

When asked to choose the greatest Husker player of all time, players were more reluctant to name just one. A strong feeling expressed by many was the impossibility of comparing players from different eras. More than one pre–World War II era Husker expressed the belief that so many of the greats of his era and before, men like Chamberlin, Sauer, Cardwell, and others, would be even better if they had the training and equipment available to players today. Others pointed out the difficulties in comparing two-way players and today's specialists. With all these reservations noted, the usual names continually pop up. Weir, Cardwell, Chamberlin, Sauer, Rozier, Novak, Francis, Reynolds, and Rodgers all received a fair number of votes. Other players also gained mention by more than one former Cornhusker. Wayne Meylan, Charles Brock, Turner Gill, and Bob Brown found supporters. Herb Dewitz provides an example of the very personal memories that go into making such a decision. His choice for

41. Wayne Meylan's crushing tackle against Oklahoma State caused a Cowboy fumble. Courtesy of the University of Nebraska Archives

the greatest all-time Husker player was Raymond "Bub" Weller, a tackle on the 1920–22 teams. Dewitz's reasoning was simple and straightforward: "I played behind him and hardly ever had to make a tackle. He got 'em first."

All-Opponent teams are always good for generating controversy and sparking memories. Former Cornhuskers all have their favorite opponents, the ones that hit them harder and ran past them faster than anyone else. Again, when queried, these players came up with names that range from the familiar to the unknown, and each had a reason for his choice. Gayle Sayers, Billy Sims, Bernie Kosar, Steve Sloan, Nile Kinnick, Leroy Selmon all have their fans. Leon Hart from Notre Dame, Paul Christman of Missouri, Frankie Albert from Stanford, and Steve Owens of Oklahoma are close behind the first group. Some of the others may require one to search his memory a little harder to picture the player. Jack Ashburn feels that Harold Stebbins of the 1938 Pittsburgh team was "the hardest runner I ever played against." Looking back on the years 1940–42, Marvin Athey voted for Dick Wildung, a tackle from the University of Minnesota. Athey felt Wildung "reminded me of how Ed Weir must have played at Nebraska." Ritch Bahe was impressed by Jim Backus from Oklahoma. "Backus was a stonewall to block." An OU player that impressed LaVerne Torczon was Tommy McDonald. The reason for Torczon's respect: "He could run like a bullet." Running backs are always easy to remember, as the response to this question demonstrates. In addition to the runners already mentioned, players such as J. C. Caroline of Illinois, Red Franklin of Iowa, James Wilder of Missouri, Pete Peoas of Indiana, and Pete Kemetovic of Stanford earned the respect of some Cornhuskers.

Former Huskers were also asked about the impact of their playing experience on their lives. Again, a remarkable consistency permeates their responses. Paul Shields, a teammate of Guy Chamberlin, looks back over the past seventy years and concludes, "I would accept no substitute for my Nebraska experience. It affects your whole outlook on life." Edward Lanphere, who played in 1918 and 1919, recognizes that this experience has had "a deep and broad influence on every day of my life."

This appreciation of the experience does not diminish as one approaches the present day. Cynics may claim that young people today are different from their ancestors, that they don't recognize the benefits of their educational experiences. But the response of a recent former Husker, Craig Johnson (1977–81), is fairly typical. "I feel it [playing for NU] developed my attitude towards setting goals and working to accomplish them. I think it helps me relate or take in stride some of the setbacks a person can experience in the business world."

Steve Runty, who performed a few years ahead of Johnson (in 1969–73) and now is an independent businessman, expresses the same sentiments. "The experience for me was invaluable. The experience provided me with an environment which required a lot of discipline and hard work. We were required to devote a great deal of time to the program. You could never get comfortable about earning a position. This background gave me the background I needed for the business world."

Many players emphasize this correlation between the attitudes and disciplines learned on the playing field and success in their careers. Pat Fischer, a member of the national championship teams and presently a successful high school football coach and athletic director, voices the opinion that "The association with a champion makes future expectations run higher. I expect more out of myself and my employers expect more out of me because I am from the 'Nebraska Program'." A teammate of Fischer's, Keith Wortman, summarized it this way: "I'd never been on a winner in my life until I came [to Nebraska], then all of a sudden I was surrounded by them." Dick Davis, from the late 1960s, echoed the same sentiments: "When you're around quality and quality people, those things breed other motivations. Football was a tremendous confidence builder. I could say 'Hey, I can do these things' and then apply this to fifteen other things."

Larry Jacobson played on the first national championship team and was the first Nebraska recipient of the Outland Trophy. Today, as a vice president of Dean, Witter, Reynolds, Jacobson has nothing but praise for his Nebraska experience. "I feel that football gave me the confidence to attack other experience in my life. It gave me name recognition to give me a start in my business." This second point can't be overemphasized. Rex Fischer, Pat's uncle and another member of the 1955 Orange Bowl team, is a practicing obstetrician/gynecologist in Manhattan, Kansas, and is quite blunt about this factor. "It is an asset to former players to have that recognition of being a former player."

With a smile, Adrian Fiala had to agree with the Fischers and Jacobson. Adrian missed by one season playing on the national champion teams but likes to point out that his years (1966–70) laid the groundwork for those teams. Adrian now practices law in Lincoln and admits that "being a Husker has had a very significant influence on my life. People still remember you and your playing days. It's really interesting to walk into a meeting room or a judge's chamber and find that the first words often spoken are 'Well, how's the football team going to do this year?' Hard to believe, but true."

Some players are more philosophical about the impact of their days at Nebraska. They see it in a broader light. LaVerne Torczon, a member of the Orange Bowl team of 1955 and later an All-Pro lineman in the American Football League, sees his days as a Husker "as a stepping stone to my life of this date. It taught me how to be a man and assume responsibility." Wayne Blue, a member of the 1941 Rose Bowl squad, echoes this thought: "My football experiences provided me with the basic knowledge of the future trials and tribulations of life—the victories, the defeats, the disappointments—all these that come in all walks of life."

Kent McCloughan, an All-Big Eight halfback in 1964 and later an All-AFC cornerback with the Oakland Raiders, is another one who recognizes the broader value in the experience. "It was a growing and maturing time in my life. I had some very disappointing times at Nebraska, especially early in my career. I feel it made me a better person and competitor. I'm proud to have played at Nebraska, and proud of their program today." McCloughan's teammate, Fred Duda, put it as succinctly as possible: "I carry athletics and all my experiences [at Nebraska] throughout everything I do."

Guy Ingles, after having been a member of the national championship squad and a coach for the Cornhuskers in the 1970s, is particularly enthusiastic about his association with the program. "Looking back, having been a player and a coach at the university where it was a highly competitive atmosphere, I think my football experience was the most humanizing experience I had at the university. I learned more about people and life in that situation than in any other at the university."

Many of the players remember the hard work involved in preparing for the season. Richard Moore, who played under Bill Glassford, feels that football at Nebraska "was the hardest work I have ever done, including hot summer construction jobs and farming." Ritch Bahe, a member of the national championship teams under Bob Devaney, sees "the year-round commitment [as being] tough mentally as well as physically." However, both players realize that the end more than makes up for the struggle along the way. After commenting on the difficulty of the task, Moore concludes, "But it was a means to a worthwhile end, i.e., a B.S. degree." Ritch Bahe is "not sure the public fully understands or really realizes the commitment made by NU football players. The time and effort required for those years is great. The rewards are all worth it, but they are duly earned."

Of course, not all the memories are happy ones or positive ones. Injuries play an important part in the memories of most players. However, it is not their own injuries that players most frequently remember but those of teammates or opponents. For the players of the 1930s, memories of what might have been take precedence as they remember teammates who lost their lives in World War II. More than one player from the Rose Bowl squad, for instance, mentioned Butch Luther, the team's quarterback, and what a loss his death during the war was.

For some the memories are very personal. Charley Bryant was a member of the Orange Bowl team of 1955. Even those who criticize the performance of the Huskers on that day, and there are many, recognize the consistently solid performance turned in by Bryant. Throughout that entire season, his line play was the subject of laudatory comments and articles. When asked what he remembers most about those years as a Husker, Bryant, a black, replies, "I had to stay in a separate hotel in Missouri and Oklahoma." The Big Seven and the states in which its institutions were located were not all ready to grant equality to all individuals, no matter how talented they may have been.

To anyone who has been part of a team—athletic, business, military, or otherwise—the comment of Pat Fischer should have a special ring. On any successful team, a special camaraderie develops. This sense of belonging, of accomplishing goals through joint efforts, is something that can be found nowhere else. At some point that relationship must end. Pat Fischer recognized that. When asked what his saddest memory of his days as a Husker was, he replied, "sitting in front of my locker during my senior year realizing that it was all going to be over in a short time."

Many wish to continue in the game. Former NU Recruiting Coordinator Steve Pederson mentions the aspirations of high school ball players. Ursula Walsh cites the struggle she had as academic counselor to convince players that pro ball wasn't for most of them and that education was therefore a necessity. Even the former players who have gone on to successful careers outside of football remember that it took several seasons at Nebraska before they realized that pro ball was not the end-all of their existence. Adrian Fiala listed the educational opportunities as one of the reasons for attending NU but readily admits that for his first two or three years in the program, "when anyone asked me what my plans were after college, I always told them to play in the pros."

Such dreams of professional football were not as commonplace or as realistic for players of an earlier generation. Sed Hartmann, the running back from the early 1920s, remembers being offered $50 a game by the Green Bay Packers after he graduated from Nebraska. He simply couldn't afford to take them up on their offer, especially since if you were injured "you went home. They didn't have any kind of insurance or anything."

In the late 1930s, the Chicago Bears offered Bob Mehring $1,500 per season to play for them. He attempts to downplay this offer by citing the successful record a number of former Nebraska players had had with the team. Link Lyman was one of the all-time Bear greats, and, according to Mehring, "All it took was a word from Link and you were given a chance." Mehring felt he had to turn down the Bears' offer. Not only did he think he could do better financially in another line of work, his experiences in the College All-Star game had convinced him that, at 170 pounds, he was no match physically for the pros.

Right after World War II, professional football still didn't have the allure that it does today. Upon his discharge from the Navy, Al Zikmund returned to the family home in Ord. He began getting phone calls from George Halas, the owner of the Chicago Bears of the National Football League, and from the New

York Titans of the rival All-America Conference trying to convince him to give their teams a try. Over a period of two weeks, first one team would call and then the other. It turned into a bidding war. Of course, the Zikmund home was on a party line and Al remembers getting a lot of advice from the family's neighbors about what he should do. Finally, the Titans dropped out after Halas offered an $8,000 annual contract. Al admits that this was an excellent deal for the times. But, since he was married with a small child, he felt he had to turn it down. After discussing it with his wife, she convinced him that he should return to the university and get his master's degree so he could become a teacher, a job with security.

Today, athletes are still faced with such decisions but the stakes have changed. For many, a professional contract is worth too much money to turn down. Every year stories appear of players who put off medical school or law school or graduate school for a chance at the pros. Even a brief stint on the big league level could provide the financing for the dream home or the dream career. Not only are professional contracts worth more money today, professional sports have expanded to include more teams carrying more players than was the case twenty or thirty or, certainly, fifty, years ago. The odds are better that a Nebraska player can make it to the pros and, when he does, he will be a much wealthier young man.

Looking back over the years and the comments, one can't help but be impressed with the enthusiasm with which former players speak of the program. The memories and the experiences continue to motivate, to inspire, and to give pleasure to the participants. Al Zikmund, perhaps, put it best. Playing football for the University of Nebraska is "an experience that molds your life. You come out of it with something." While disappointments existed, the overwhelming majority would agree with Kelly Saalfeld, who simply stated: "If I had it to do over again, I wouldn't change a thing."

Chapter Eleven

The Dream Continues

The success that Nebraska enjoyed in the past was dependent upon the proper mix of coaches and athletes. At the present time, with Tom Osborne at the helm, the coaching side of the equation is well covered. Attracting quality athletes to the university is what will determine the future of Big Red football. If Nebraska has a legitimate chance for the national championship in the future, it must continue to draw the best players possible.

Much has been made of the desire of young boys from Nebraska to grow up and play for Big Red. Tom Morrow, a senior walk-on offensive tackle in 1984, was quoted in *Sports Illustrated* about why he came to Nebraska: "Nebraska football is *the* thing in this state. That's just the way it is." Although there is a great deal of truth to this, the project of recruiting talented athletes to play for Nebraska is an enormous one. Tom Osborne wants to make one point very clear. "Recruiting is a lot harder than some Nebraskans think. They feel it is a given that great football players would want to come here to play football. That isn't always the case." He feels that recruiting is the most important aspect of a successful program because good athletes make good coaches. However, recruiting is also hard work. It can be a very trying experience. Bob Devaney recognized that. "Recruiting is a fickle business. You never know what it is that causes a 17-year-old kid who is highly sought after by a number of colleges to pick one over the other."

The man responsible for the management of this effort at Nebraska during the mid-1980s was Steve Pederson. Although Steve resigned in March 1986 to pursue opportunities in private business, there is no one better able to describe the effort and the considerations that go into offering a high school senior the opportunity to play for the Cornhuskers.

The Nebraska recruiting effort leaves nothing to chance. A definite strategy guides the program. Electronic wizardry may have enhanced the ability to track and plot the careers of high school athletes, but a lot of elbow grease still goes into making the program work.

Pederson explained how Nebraska gains information on potential recruits. A

42. Husker cocaptains in 2005. Photo by Dan Dulaney

popular misconception, he feels, is that alumni and fans play a role in uncovering talent. Very rarely, if ever, is a recruit found this way. The key to a successful program is in establishing a relationship with the high school coaches. One of the real strengths of the NU recruiting effort is the stability of the staff. Coach Osborne pointed this out in his book. "The stability of our staff has allowed us to have great continuity in our recruiting. Each coach gets to know the high school coaches and athletes well in his assigned geographic area." These men on the high school level are the ones who supply the names of outstanding athletes. Nebraska also subscribes to a scouting service, but uses this more as a starting point rather than as an end.

Another popular misconception is that talented high school athletes are courted as early as their freshman and sophomore years. Although this may be true at some institutions, Nebraska doesn't really begin any contact until the end of the student's junior year. At this time approximately three thousand athletes receive questionnaires from the recruiting staff. If the athlete is interested, and returns the questionnaire, his responses are evaluated by Steve and the various position coaches. The timing of this initial mailing is also the result of a deliberate strategy. Physical development is an important element in football and studies have shown that much of the growth in a boy's body takes place during his high school days. A philosophical consideration also influences the timing. "We feel earlier contact is a distraction to these kids," said Pederson. "The athlete needs to enjoy his high school years and do well in school. He doesn't need college coaches bothering him."

By the end of the summer, a workable list of six hundred or so athletes has been developed. Now the serious work begins. Jack Pierce, the assistant coach whose primary responsibility is recruiting, goes on the road from August 1 until the national signing date in February. Five days a week he crosses the country, trying to see all these players and to evaluate their abilities. The other assistant coaches also try to sneak out for a couple of days during the season to scout some high school games. Meanwhile, film is being studied back in Lincoln. The potential recruit isn't lost in the shuffle, though. "The player receives something in the mail from us each week from August 1 to the National Signing Date—sometimes more than one item a week."

Somehow, that list must be reduced to about 120 by the first of December. This is the date that the NCAA stipulates for the beginning of personal visits. At Nebraska this means that the coaches, in addition to what has become an annual preparation for a bowl game, must start to hit the road and personally visit these prospective recruits. Even Tom Osborne travels the circuit. Steve Pederson noted that Osborne has specific candidates in mind for these trips. "He is out seeing players we know we want to invite in for visits, that we know are outstanding football players that we want to come to the University of Nebraska. He gets into the home of every player we invite for a visit at least once and sometimes twice."

Due to National Collegiate Athletic Association regulations limiting the number of assistant coaches in a program and limiting recruiting trips to assistant coaches, Steve Pederson, as recruiting coordinator, wasn't allowed to recruit off campus, but that doesn't mean he wasn't busy. To start with, his job would have been a lot easier if he could have had a telephone surgically implanted in his ear. He was constantly on the phone following up on information, scheduling visits for Jack Pierce, arranging for campus visits by potential scholarship recipients, and the countless other tasks he had to perform. All the information he gathered was placed on computers for easy access. Easy, of course, is a relative word.

How can you distinguish among so many talented players? Is the key the time in the "40"? Or is it body size? How about the potential for development? Maybe Player A is as big and fast as he will ever get while Player B, with the help of the NU strength program, could add another thirty or forty pounds and drop his speed in the "40". While this isn't easy to determine, there's another variable. How about the grades?

One thing Nebraska prides itself on is the graduation rate of its players. Pederson felt it was important to determine if a recruit has the ability to undertake a college study program. Again, come the variables. Is this individual a poor student or simply one who hasn't had a lot of opportunity to excel? Could he benefit from the academic counseling at the university? Should we take the risk? Then, finally, comes the real intangible. How do you measure heart, desire? Has he the type of character that we want at Nebraska?

The bottom line is that Nebraska will award an average of twenty scholarships in any given year. To start with three thousand potential recipients and wind up with twenty certainly requires a great deal of effort, talent, and, although Steve never used the word, a little bit of luck.

One of the most important aspects of the whole recruiting process is the campus visit. NCAA rules allow the candidate to spend no more than forty-eight hours on campus. Each year approximately ninety-five high school seniors find out how much can be crammed into forty-eight hours. A potential recruit has time to meet with Coach Osborne, Strength Coach Boyd Epley, the academic counselor for the team, and faculty members from his areas of academic interest. The visit is important, not only so that the coaching staff can get a better evaluation of the player, but so the player can get a better view of the university and the geographical area where he may be spending an important part of his life. So concerned about this aspect is the Athletic Department that it arranges Saturday luncheons with local community leaders to allow the prospective recruit to learn more about Lincoln and Omaha. You realize, after looking at what goes on during one of these weekends, that Steve was not exaggerating when he said: "At Nebraska, we approach a recruit's visit as an educational experience."

After all the evaluation and the visits, the hard choices have to be made. Nebraska must determine to whom scholarships will be offered, and those offered the scholarships must decide whether or not to accept them. It is a tense and a maddening time for the coaches as they await the final decisions. On the one hand, there is relief when a sought-after recruit signs. That ends it for the athlete. He has made his decision and now must work as hard as he can to maximize the opportunity. On the other hand, the coach won't know for several years whether he made the right decision. It won't be until the player is a junior or a senior that the answer to the question of whether or not he should have been offered a scholarship will be given. That is why, Steve said, Nebraska always seeks out the best athletes. If players are awarded scholarships on the basis of their high school position, they could outgrow that position or find another position for which they are better suited. Also, the needs of the NU football team change. It is difficult to know how many quarterbacks or linebackers will be needed in four or five years. Therefore, recruiting the best athletes means there will always be someone ready to play.

Coach Osborne points out the consequences of such decisions. "You go out and recruit 20 players a year and some years you're lucky and 15 of those players do well—hopefully they become fine players. Another year you recruit 20 and only 5 of them pan out. It's always a calculated risk that you take and if you have two years in a row that only five of them pan out, pretty soon you're a .500 football team."

Junior college and walk-on recruiting are handled differently because the philosophy is different. Nebraska recruits junior college players to fill specific needs. Since, in all likelihood, a junior college recruit will have only two years of varsity eligibility remaining, his contribution must be immediate or the scholarship will have been wasted. So, when NU goes after junior college players, it looks for something different than it would with a high school recruit. Perhaps because of injuries or withdrawals from the program, a shortage of defensive backs or linebackers exists. The scouts then go to the junior colleges and seek individuals who can be defensive backs or linebackers. This can't be a yearly event, however. Steve feels that "the secret of having a successful program is to have replacements within the system. If you are recruiting a lot of junior college players that means you aren't doing a good job recruiting the high school players." At best, junior college recruiting is "a shortstop method."

Walk-ons have a grand tradition at Nebraska. As Tom Osborne once put it, "I guess we're sort of the mecca of walk-ons." Jack McCallum, writing in *Sports Illustrated*, tried to explain it:

Without doubt, the No. 1 reason a walk-on walks on is intense loyalty to a particular institution. He may have other scholarship offers, but if he has been dreaming of playing for good ol' State U his whole life, then that's where he's going to play, even if he has to pay his own way. That kind of devotion is the reason Nebraska, the quintessential State U., stands helmet and cleats above the rest in making walk-ons an integral part of the program.

He went on to note that 90 to 95 percent of Husker walk-ons are in-state products "who simply wanted to play for Nebraska from the time they made their first crab block in booties."

Legends are made by individuals who walked on and became heroes. Once again, the reality is somewhat less romantic. Walk-ons are scouted and recruited. They may be individuals who appear to have great potential but haven't yet realized it. They may be athletes who played one position in high school and might blossom if moved to a new position. They may be the proverbial "late bloomers" who didn't show that much promise in their high school careers but toward the end looked as if they might be good.

In an average year, Nebraska receives over three hundred requests to walk on. These requests must be evaluated and decisions made. It would be physically impossible to allow that many candidates to walk on. Nebraska extends approximately sixty invitations a year for players to walk on. Once on campus and in the program, they receive treatment no different from the scholarship

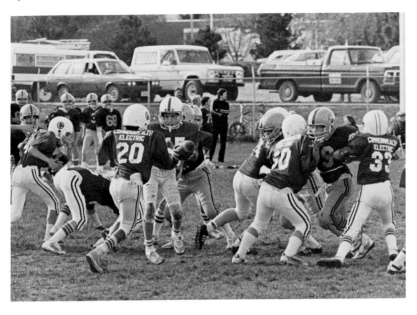

players. The tradition continues that every year some walk-ons are awarded scholarships for their performance. Nebraskans are duly proud of the walk-on tradition, but it should never be taken solely as the result of "luck."

A lot has been made about the "character" of Nebraska teams. Coach Osborne has noted, "We've generally been able to attract players who not only have ability but who also have excellent character and work habits." Although this is difficult to quantify, both Steve Pederson and Ursula Walsh have some pretty specific ideas about what it means. Talking about incoming players, the former recruiting coordinator noted: "When they come here, they're normally pretty serious about achieving all they can athletically and academically. We get guys who are pretty serious about their education."

Both comment on the recruits' capacity for hard work. Partly this is the midwestern influence, but also it is the reputation of the program itself. As Dr. Walsh put it, "If they're into the party life, they're probably not going to choose us anyway." Nebraska doesn't have the ocean or the mountains nearby. You know what you are coming here for. Secondly, because of the influence of Tom Osborne, recruits are aware that academics are an important aspect of the program. Dr. Walsh emphasizes this again and again. "The coaches automatically begin with academics in their recruiting presentations—because of Tom's stress. If you aren't serious about getting a college education, Nebraska probably wouldn't be attractive to you."

Frank Solich, offensive backfield coach, has seen this change since his days as a player at Nebraska in the early 1960s. He feels that the limitation of the number of times a recruit can be visited at his home (three) limits how well he can get to know the coaches, and therefore other factors influence his decision. "A majority of the recruits will look at the institution, itself, in terms of the quality of education, type of programs, graduation rate of athletes, academic counseling program. I think that the players are much more aware of the

43–45. The boys get bigger, but the dream remains the same—to play for the Cornhuskers. Photos by Dan Dulaney

46. The crew that leads the cheers. Photo by Dan Dulaney

education factor and all that surrounds it than maybe players were in my day."

Of course, Solich isn't so naive as to think academics are the only factor that recruits analyze. Physical facilities are important. Most recruits have been exposed to weight training and want to see how NU stacks up in that department. For some, the decision rests on how well the program will prepare them to play professional football. This last consideration could be a misleading one, however. Jim Benagh, in *Making It to #1*, estimates that the odds are 12,500 to 1 against a high school football player making it to the pros.

Guy Ingles, who played and coached at Nebraska for over a decade, has the same view. His insight is particularly interesting due to his additional experience as backfield coach at North Texas State University and North Carolina State University. Now a financial consultant in Omaha, Guy feels that recruits today "have more choices and more factors involved in their decisions" than when he was recruited. As a coach, "you have to sell the total environment and situation—the education, the off season conditioning and weight training— the more human aspects."

Most recruits recognize that a life exists after football and want to be prepared for it. This type of thinking goes along with the overall attitude of the Nebraska players. Dr. Walsh looked at potential recruits with a certain interest in mind. "I want to see if they're like us—conservative, stable, hard-working—all the Protestant work ethic kinds of things that pretty aptly describe this program." Dr. Walsh isn't alone in that type of evaluation of the Nebraska program. As far back as 1968, *Sports Illustrated* used that attitude to characterize the Nebraska program. "Solid is the word for Nebraska. Solid God-fearing farmers. Solid Republican politics. Solid spine-jarring football. Solid red is the color scheme of the University's Memorial Stadium on Model T Street in Lincoln and solid sellout is what its seats [are] in the Fall."

Certainly, the recruitment of athletes seems to be in good hands. But, what about the future of the program? Sports columnists and observers have recently been speculating on the continued enthusiasm of the recruits themselves. Such speculation usually centers around maintaining the interest of recruits in college athletics. Longer seasons, extended practices, pressure to win—all seem to be adding to the burden carried by the student athlete. Given the time he must devote to the football program and the commitment required by his academic load, the student athlete doesn't have a great deal of free time to engage in social activities or to pursue part-time employment to earn some spending money.

Frank Solich confirms the growth in time commitment. When asked to compare his era (1963–65) with the present day, Coach Solich observed: "Football seems to be a year-round proposition anymore. To be successful, you can't avoid a year-round commitment." Ursula Walsh also had an interesting comment. She feels that many fans don't realize how hard the players work. In her mind, "It is a pick and shovel job." To illustrate this, she referred to a former player who had been a math major. As a project, he had at one time figured how many hours a week football grant-in-aid recipients had to devote to their studies, training, and game preparation. The conclusion, she feels, is startling. "A free ride is worth about $.75 an hour."

Perhaps because of the publicity this topic has received, or because of perceptions developed elsewhere, many of the players from earlier eras offered the same comment: "I don't think [college football players] today are having fun anymore." Such comments were usually followed by "it has become too much of a business," or "money is too important today," or "they just don't let them go out and play anymore." Those involved with the game today would disagree with such conclusions.

George Sullivan, who has been associated with the Nebraska program over the last four decades, is one of those who feels that players today are enjoying themselves. He prefaces his remarks by stating, "I don't think anybody really enjoys getting bruised and torn up. It's more the camaraderie." While conceding that the players today are more regimented than when he first joined the program, Sully "can't believe they dislike it." His conclusion is that the

47–49. Local boy makes good. Hometown pride swells each season in Memorial Stadium. Photos by Dan Dulaney

enjoyment factor grows after the playing days are finished. "Memories are the big thing. The times get better the more distant they are." Frank Solich echoed the same comment: "To some degree it [fun] relates to perception. As the years pass the pleasant memories get stronger." He feels the number of players participating in the program offers evidence of the enjoyment. "You have to enjoy it to put in all that time and effort. If the fun isn't there, you're going to get out of it."

Former players Guy Ingles and Adrian Fiala, both of whom have remained close to the program, second Solich's comments. Adrian is the only one to

admit a small reduction in enjoyment. "The 'big stakes' involved have," in his mind, "taken some of the fun out of it." But, "if the athlete didn't enjoy it, he wouldn't be out there doing it." Guy Ingles summarized all the reasons he thinks it is still fun. "It's fun because it is a unique competitive situation where you have to use your head and your heart and your body and you must keep focused. I don't think you'd have as many players playing [football] today if it wasn't fun."

Tom Osborne has a different view. While emphasizing that players today are enjoying themselves, he offers another perspective. "I think there is a certain satisfaction that a person gets from doing something well and achieving. I think if a person enjoys achievement and enjoys knowing where he stands, enjoys really working at something, that there is probably more of that type of enjoyment today than there ever was." As for off-the-field fun, Coach Osborne believes that hasn't changed at all. The friendships, the camaraderie, are still present.

When contemplating the future, one thing that doesn't worry Steve Pederson, or anyone connected with the Nebraska program, is increased enforcement of NCAA regulations. In fact, he welcomes it. Given Nebraska's record of compliance and the integrity with which the whole program operates, Pederson feels that the Cornhuskers could only benefit from such efforts. The reduction in under-the-table payments and other illegal offerings allegedly so common at other institutions would allow the recruit to focus on the pluses of a program, and Nebraska is highly competitive in this area.

One matter that does concern the former recruiting coordinator is the continuing erosion of the university's budget. The financial status of the University of Nebraska has a direct bearing on his recruiting efforts. Because of the importance of a quality education to many of the recruits, Steve wonders if the University will stay competitive in this area. For instance, he expressed disappointment over attempts to close the Sheldon Art Gallery. He wonders what impact it would have on a potential scholarship recipient to be told that there were only two major art galleries in the entire state and that one of them had been forced to curtail service.

When all the variables are figured in, how does the future look? Can the University of Nebraska continue to attract quality athletes? Can the fans expect competitive teams year after year? In *More Than Winning*, Coach Osborne offers some sobering thoughts for Nebraska fans: "athletics is always cyclical. Nobody wins forever, and this will be true of Nebraska. We've been fortunate to have a long-lasting cycle, however."

Adrian Fiala cautions against putting too much faith in the physical facilities or the won-loss record of the coaches. When contemplating the future success of the program, he feels that "It's not just the *x*'s and *o*'s that make the program great—it's the people." As noted in an earlier chapter, it isn't only the head coach but the assistant coaches who make a difference. Under Bob Devaney and Tom Osborne, there has been a great deal of stability, far above the national average, among the assistants at Nebraska. This makes coaching easier because new coaches don't have to be taught the system before they can teach it to the players. The continuing quest for the national championship also contributes to the coaching stability. Time and time again, the comment was made that the current group of coaches "wants to win the national championship." People close to the program recognize that several of the assistants aspire to head coaching positions but feel they have an uncompleted mission here. Once that goal is achieved, there could be an exodus. The same observers cite the loyalty of the assistants to Coach Osborne and offer the opinion that, if he were to retire or move on, many of the assistants would also leave the program.

Thus the key seems to be the people involved. While stating that "every day recruiting becomes more competitive. There's a lot more parity in college football [today]," Steve Pederson feels assured of one thing. "I think we have a tremendous football coach right now and most of the program centers on what he has done. Without him, I can't tell you what the future will be. With him I feel fairly certain that the future of Nebraska football will be very good. That he will continue to do things the right way." Thus the conclusion of the majority is that as long as Tom Osborne is the head coach, Nebraska will have a model program that annually challenges the best. But, as Guy Ingles cautions, "After Tom, that remains to be seen; but it's hard for me to believe that the program would be as good or better."

Is this true? How do the two men most intimately connected with Nebraska's success feel about this? Here the future looks a little more optimistic. Tom Osborne stresses the cyclical nature of the sport but softens that by noting the tradition, facilities, and fan support enjoyed by the Cornhuskers. Such attributes aid the perpetuation of a program, although "it's not automatic." He concludes by offering the opinion that "I think Nebraska is in a better situation than a lot of schools but there are schools that are in as good or better situations."

Bob Devaney, the original architect of the program, is the first to credit Tom Osborne's contribution and influence. "As long as Tom stays here our football program will be at the top. He's a great football coach. Tom's the finest football coach I have ever known—as far as all aspects of the program are concerned." As for after Tom Osborne leaves the program, Coach Devaney remains optimistic. "If we can keep top flight people in our coaching positions and if these people don't get complacent, we'll be OK." Given the accomplishments of the athletic administration over the past three decades, Nebraska fans can feel comfortable that the right people will be in those positions and will be directing the Cornhuskers toward continued national prominence.

Record is for league play

1907	Missouri Valley Conference Champions 1–0–0
1910	Missouri Valley Conference Champions 2–0–0
1911	Missouri Valley Conference Champions 2–0–1
1912	Missouri Valley Conference Co-Champions 2–0–0 (Tied with Iowa State)
1914	Missouri Valley Conference Champions 3–0–0
1915	Missouri Valley Conference Champions 4–0–0
1916	Missouri Valley Conference Champions 3–1–0
1917	Missouri Valley Conference Champions 2–0–0
1921	Missouri Valley Conference Champions 3–0–0
1922	Missouri Valley Conference Champions 5–0–0
1923	Missouri Valley Conference Champions 3–0–2
1928	Big Six Conference Champions 5–0–0
1929	Big Six Conference Champions 3–0–2
1931	Big Six Conference Champions 5–0–0
1932	Big Six Conference Champions 5–0–0
1933	Big Six Conference Champions 5–0–0
1935	Big Six Conference Champions 4–0–1
1936	Big Six Conference Champions 5–0–0
1937	Big Six Conference Champions 3–0–2
1940	Big Six Conference Champions 5–0–0
1963	Big Eight Conference Champions 7–0–0
1964	Big Eight Conference Champions 6–1
1965	Big Eight Conference Champions 7–0–0
1966	Big Eight Conference Champions 6–1–0
1969	Big Eight Conference Co-Champions 6–1–0 (Tied with Missouri)
1970	Big Eight Conference Champions 7–0–0 National Champions
1971	Big Eight Conference Champions 7–0 National Champions
1972	Big Eight Conference Champions 5–1–1
1975	Big Eight Conference Co-Champions 6–1–0 (Tied with Oklahoma)
1978	Big Eight Conference Co-Champions 6–1–0 (Tied with Oklahoma)
1981	Big Eight Conference Champions 7–0–0
1982	Big Eight Conference Champions 7–0–0
1983	Big Eight Conference Champions 7–0–0
1984	Big Eight Conference Co-Champions 6–1 (Tied with Oklahoma)

Nebraska's Champions

A Big Red Bibliography

Denney, James, Hollis Limprecht, and Howard Silber. *Go Big Red*. Omaha: Kratville Publications, 1971.

Devaney, Bob (and Friends). *Devaney*. Lincoln: By the Author, 1981.

Greunke, Lowell R. *Big Red Trivia Quiz Book*. Omaha: La Donna Press, 1984.

Israel, David. *The Cornhuskers: Nebraska Football*. Chicago: Henry Regnery Co., 1975.

Limprecht, Hollis J., James Denney, and Howard Silber. *Bob Devaney: Portrait of a Winner*. Chicago: Kratville Publications, 1972.

McCallum, John D. *Big Eight Football*. New York: Charles Scribner's Sons, 1979.

Okerlund, David. *The Big Red Machine*. Lincoln: John E. Tate, 1976.

Osborne, Tom (with John C. Roberts). *More Than Winning*. Nashville: Thomas Nelson Publishers, 1985.

Ware, Frederick. *Fifty Years of Football*. Omaha: Omaha World Herald, 1940.

Winkler, Charlie. *My Big Red Obsession*. Grand Island: Winkler Publishing Co., 1981, 1982.